Your Access Code: aaa0-b0b5-589c

The Thriving Framework
Diagnostic Tool
Where's your urgency?

Welcome to "Surviving to Thriving: A Planning Framework for
Leaders of Private Colleges and Universities." You have been
granted access to The Thriving Framework Diagnostic Tool, a
companion survey that enables leadership teams to evaluate their
own institution across the elements of the Thriving Framework.

Access is easy! Visit Thriving.CredoHigherEd.com/Login
to redeem your code.

For my husband, Keith, because he has encouraged me to fly as high as I can in my professional career, and has been the wind beneath my wings so I could!

— *Joanne Soliday*

To my wife and tandem partner, Cheri, for your courageous leadership, and to the hundreds of capable educators with whom I have had the privilege of serving over the last three decades.

— *Rick Mann*

Credo
940 Golf House Road West #200
Whitsett, NC 27377
CredoHigherEd.com
336.585.1044

Special discounts are available on quantity purchases by universities, colleges, higher education associations, and others. For details, contact the publisher at the address above.

Library of Congress Control Number: 2013954174
ISBN 978-0-61591291-2
Production Editor: Emma L. Jones
Copy Editor: Sue Pick
Cover and Interior Design: Thesis, Inc.

First Edition

Surviving to Thriving:
A Planning Framework for Leaders of Private Colleges & Universities

Joanne Soliday
& Rick Mann

Endorsements

This work will revolutionize the way we think, plan, and act in the world of private higher education. The authors take exhaustive research and years of engagement with universities and their leaders to illuminate what makes a private university thrive in this age of change and uncertainty. What is most telling is that it takes the old excuse of "we are unique" and strips it away to reveal a common framework of action that all private universities can and must follow. This book will be a must-read for faculty, administrators, board members, and alumni, as well as the parents of future students who desire the best return on their investment.
— *Dr. Mark Lombardi, President, Maryville University*

"Surviving to Thriving" is long overdue and fills a critical need for those of us leading colleges and universities. Based upon her experiences with literally hundreds of institutions, Joanne Soliday, the quintessential champion and authority of small independent colleges and universities, has written the definitive book for presidents and their senior leadership.
— *Dr. Tiffany McKillip Franks, President, Averett University*

I highly recommend this book to anyone who wants a litmus test for what is or isn't working for you as a president, for you as an administrator, and above all for you as a member of a board of trustees. This book works, and it will turn your school around.
— *Dr. Gabriel J. Zeis, T.O.R., President, Saint Francis University*

The presidency at a residential liberal arts college requires a "ministry of presence" – everywhere, always, and at all times. It can easily become overwhelming. "Surviving to Thriving" takes the many elements of this ministry and presents them in ways that are manageable and accessible – the trees are revealed in a way that the forest becomes manageable. This should be high-priority reading for every new president and a good refresher for experienced presidents eager to be renewed.

— *Dr. Richard Torgerson, President Emeritus, Luther College*

"Surviving to Thriving" is a helpful, easy-to-read "recipe for success" for anyone who aspires to the role of college or university president. Joanne's years of experience in higher education are readily evident in this practical book for leaders in education. The role of CEO is fraught with pitfalls and potential rewards. Joanne has a way of helping the reader navigate through the confusion with a focus on success in a complicated profession. I only wish she had written the book two decades ago!

— *Dr. David Joyce, President, Brevard College*

"Surviving to Thriving" is a tremendous resource for presidents, boards of trustees, and all leadership team members of small, private colleges. Joanne Soliday and Rick Mann capture the heart that is the life-changing nature of this education. They outline critical strategies to address the challenges small campuses face, and to strengthen and position a campus for long-term success.

— *Dr. A. Hope Williams, President, North Carolina Independent Colleges and Universities*

Joanne Soliday has built a tremendous wealth of knowledge about the optimal inner workings of colleges and universities, accumulated over years of experience with a wide range of higher education institutions. She has always been a "go-to" person for me. In "Surviving to Thriving," just as Joanne has done in the past, she balances the realistic with the aspirational, the strategic with the tactical, the procedural with the substantive, the cultural with the functional, and the today with the tomorrow.

— *Dr. Jonathan Brand, President, Cornell College*

Higher education has navigated a vast array of cycles and challenges over the last half century or so, but today we face issues of rapid change like no other: new learning modalities, the twin forces of technology and globalism, the fragility of enrollments and student retention, highly competitive demands in market niche and branding, critical issues of academic governance, and an unprecedented public demand to demonstrate our worth as institutions of higher education. Consequently, decision making is necessitated at a pace heretofore unknown within the academy. Little wonder that many colleges and universities are in a retrenchment or even survival mode. Joanne Soliday and Rick Mann, from their lifetime perspective as seasoned and respected educators, have offered us a most timely and invaluable template for thriving through the leadership of our private colleges and universities. Their nine drivers for success are highly relevant, thoughtfully presented, practical and accessible, and are an indispensable blueprint for leadership in our brave new world of higher education.

— *Dr. Doug Orr, President Emeritus, Warren Wilson College*

Joanne Soliday and Rick Mann have produced a relevant and practical private higher education leadership book that is a "must read" for many audiences. "Surviving to Thriving" is a meaningful and adaptable framework that all students in higher education programs should read and discuss. This book is also a targeted road map for administrators working in both upper-level and mid-level management. The challenges for private higher education will continue to increase in the years to come. There will be some colleges and universities that will not survive. The authors of this book pour their knowledge and souls into helping all of us who love and want to protect the unique qualities of private higher education. They have provided a solid and well-tested planning framework that will guide administrators beyond just surviving.

— *Dr. Pamela Balch, President, West Virginia Wesleyan College*

In "Surviving to Thriving," Joanne Soliday conveys with extraordinary passion her unshakable belief in the critical role small private colleges play in developing in students the qualities of mind and character needed for success in the 21st century. Joanne's legacy in higher education will endure through the powerful framework outlined in this insightful book and through the careers of thousands of private college leaders who have had the privilege of working with her.

— *Dr. Barbara Farley, President, Illinois College*

Presidential search committees should make this book required reading to better understand the intellect, passion, drive, and collaborative spirit necessary for an engaged and forward thinking leader.

— *Dr. Bill Fleming, President, Palm Beach Atlantic University*

Drawing upon an immense well of experience and success, Joanne provides a solid and grounded focus for the president willing to work hard and to make a difference. Such a president could well maintain clarity and sense of purpose by keeping her chapter titles visible daily and her book readily available for reference. Her warmth and professionalism provide challenge laced with reassurance, essential nourishment for presidents in the midst of their busy lives. Her productive impact on my own presidency began early and continues today!

— *Dr. Norval C. Kneten, President, Barton College*

At a time when most small colleges are under siege on multiple fronts, Joanne Soliday brings an antidote to institutional anxiety in the form of a tried and true recipe for student and institutional success. Her passion for student achievement gives life to a vision and a strategy for taking struggling institutions to ones that flourish. There are few higher education leaders that have both her wisdom and her unfailing optimism.

— *Dr. Mary Meehan, President, Alverno College*

Acknowledgements

Joanne Soliday

When you start to think of the acknowledgements for a book and you don't know that you will ever write another one, you begin to think about not only the book itself, but also the encouragement along the path of your career. I have tried to say a special thank you to those who were involved in both.

I must start with thanks to colleagues who have been unconditionally supportive over a period of 30 years. Dr. Gerry Francis at Elon University has been a mentor, friend, and strategic problem solver for me throughout my career in higher education. He was instrumental in giving me the confidence to consult, and has been there every step of the way as we developed helpful tools for private colleges and universities. Dr. A. Hope Williams, Executive Director of the North Carolina Independent Colleges Association, has been instrumental in helping me understand the issues that all private colleges face today. She is a true leader in the advocacy of private colleges, and I have loved sharing our passion for them with her over the years. These two people have been amazing friends and colleagues.

A very special thank you to Rick Mann, for having the most profound effect on getting me started by telling me to select the most important topic headings and "write a few sentences" under each. I am amazed at how that jumpstarted the process for me! Also, many thanks for adding the depth of research to the book by thoroughly investigating everything I felt intuitionally.

This book could never have been written without the support of Emma Jones and Ryan Morabito, my dedicated colleagues at Credo. As our tireless marketing team, they pushed and pushed for it to happen, and Emma's unbelievable ability to find my voice in writing has been a true gift to me. When my confidence was at an all time low, theirs was high! Dr. Bryant Hudson also deserves special mention for his blessing and hard work on the survey that accompanies the book. It will be a huge factor in the research we can gather and share about thriving colleges, and we could not have considered it without him.

Thank you to Trudi Cary, who has held all of the small pieces of our business and my personal life in her hands for many years and has never, ever hesitated when I needed her to do anything to make my life or my job easier.

Special thanks to the Executive Management Team at Credo: Ryan Morabito for his consistent encouragement, Dr. Joretta Nelson for the expertise that has propelled us to another level of excellence, Allan Michler for his uncompromising loyalty, Tim Fuller for his continued ability to keep things in "context" for me, and especially to Bill Fahrner, for ALWAYS being there in the good times and the tough times as a steady, trustworthy friend and colleague. Immeasurable thanks to Tom Gavic for leading us all with a servant's heart and a quest for new opportunities that stretched me to new business horizons.

Thank you to Credo team members Dr. Dean Rodeheaver, Kevin Rolling, Dawn Rolling, and Carolyn Glime for sharing their passion and expertise about transformative environments – their input was crucial in shaping that chapter.

Thanks to former Credo leadership team member David Mee for being there at the beginning and helping to establish so much of our current credibility with private colleges.

Also, special thanks to Susan Disher and Heather Stuart, two former full-time Credo team members who were so instrumental in my ability to believe that I had something to say.

To the rest of the Credo team! I have loved working with you and appreciate each and every one of you so much. At the time of this writing, our team is a very special one. Thank you to Jennifer Hricik, Will Lee, Ryan Krier, Amy Schwalbach, Laura Fabry, Kate Vigneau, Sharon Morton, Dawn Shriver, Thayle Heggie, Aeriel Miller, Jasmine Gregory, Matt Lackey, and Ragan Riddle.

My heartfelt thanks to those along the way who tried to help me discover the best way to make this book happen. To Nan Perkins for being honest and helping me see that you just don't sit down and write, you find your style and allow your personality to shine through in your work. To Tim Riddle, for continuous encouragement about this endeavor, and for setting up tons of video equipment and taping me, to see if that might be a way to light a spark!

Sincere thanks to our wonderful partners in the production of this book – Sue Pick for her careful editing work in tandem with Emma; Mark Cook and his team at Thesis, Inc. for layout and design; and Lisa Weaver and Hickory Printing Solutions for putting ink to paper and sending this book out into the world.

Thank you to all of the college presidents who have trusted me over the years and believed that a partnership could be more important than "buying a product." With special thanks to Dr. Fred Young, former president of Elon University, for believing in a naïve young woman and appointing me to a dean's position early in my career.

I must offer gratitude to some key institutions who we visited and interviewed in the early days of building the Thriving Framework, and who participated in our initial presentations of it at NAICU and CIC: Maryville University, Messiah College, Ripon College, and St. Norbert College.

Sincere thanks also to the institutions who piloted our initial Thriving Framework Inventory diagnostic tool and offered their thoughtful feedback on its structure and effectiveness: Alvernia University, Aurora University, Averett University, Azusa Pacific University, Barton College, Bethel University, Brevard College, Dordt College, Eastern Nazarene College, Greensboro College, Illinois College, Louisburg College, Luther College, Manhattan Christian College, Maryville University, Messiah College, MidAmerica Nazarene University, Milligan College, Newberry College, Palm Beach Atlantic University, Roberts Wesleyan College, Schreiner University, Southern Adventist University, Spartanburg Methodist College, Spring Arbor University, St. Francis University, St. Norbert College, Tabor College, University of Mount Union, Warner Pacific College, Wesley College, and Wisconsin Lutheran College.

And last but not least, thank you to my family. I know there have been so many times when I should have been there, and you understood my passion for education. To my parents, Peg and Joe Cadorette, who were unbelievable models for hard work and service. To Tambra, Jeremy, and Keith for being patient while we grew up as a family with a Mom who was dedicated to you AND to a career. You are the light of my life! To my sister, Sherry, who is my wisdom on many things, but especially on being a better businesswoman! To my grandchildren – Julian, Lilly, Gavin, and Christian – for always knowing that Nanny loves you even when I am not there all of the time. And to Vicki, Ray, Cami, Janice, Jeff, Joyce, Bob, Beverlea, John, Carole, and Mom Soliday for years and years of encouragement. To

Colonel Chaplain Wayne E. Soliday, Wayne A. Soliday and Joseph Cadorette who are gone but always in my heart. I love all of you so much!

I am grateful every day for my faith and the Christian foundation that sustains me, and for the people in my church who walk that road with me. Thank you all.

Dr. Rick Mann

No book goes to press without a team effort. I want to thank the Credo team for the invitation to be a part of this journey. Joanne, you have been a wonderful supporter of my work on many levels, and it has been a rich experience to work with you on this book. I have benefited so much from our work together. I also want to thank Emma Jones at Credo, who has been remarkably skilled at shepherding this project to the finish line. I have always enjoyed working on capable teams, and this has certainly been true at Credo. Senior leaders Tom Gavic, Bill Fahrner, Tim Fuller, Dr. Joretta Nelson, and Ryan Morabito have been supportive throughout our work together as well as with the broader Credo team.

I would also like to thank those I served with at Crown College who taught me so much about private higher education. My investment in this book would not have been possible without the gracious support of the leadership at Trevecca Nazarene University including President Dan Boone, Provost Steve Pusey, Associate Provost Carol Maxson, and Dean Jim Hiatt of the Skinner School of Business and Technology.

Table of Contents

Chapter 1

A Tale of Two Colleges & Two Hundred More

Joanne Soliday

My love affair with small private colleges began on the day that I set foot on the campus of West Virginia Wesleyan College. As a first generation college student, a feeling of gratefulness and anticipation overwhelmed me that day. I was farther away from home than most of my high school classmates, and ready to embark on a journey that I never believed possible. If you had spoken with my teachers and counselors at Pittsfield High School in Massachusetts back in the 1960s, they would not have identified me as someone who would fall in love with college. You could say that I was one of those students with *potential*. I certainly didn't love learning during my high school years. In fact, I would say that learning was secondary to me. Fun and activity were primary!

My West Virginia Wesleyan College experience changed all of that. From the moment I was asked to read "Liberal Education" (Doren, 1943), our freshman common reading, to the moment I opened the car door and saw my beautiful little college, I was hooked. The transformational experience that we all talk about really happened to me! All those years ago, my small private college knew what it meant to have students engaged and connected. Even though I was in a tiny town in West Virginia, I was about to see a world that I had never seen before.

The outcomes of my college experience are numerous. Because they are so close to my heart, it's not difficult for me to list them:

- I met people from other countries.
- I learned from the residence hall experience.
- I connected with professors who cared and invited me into their homes.
- I joined clubs and organizations where I learned to lead.
- I was a part of an education department that taught me how to meet people where they are.
- I was captured by the beauty of the campus, and the places inside and outside to have conversations.
- Even back in the '60s, I was afforded the opportunity to understand experiential education through student teaching.
- I learned how to communicate with people who were not like me, and were raised in different circumstances.
- I learned how to make decisions, which included making mistakes.
- I learned how to put my feelings, reflections, and insights into writing.

- I learned what it meant to do something significant through community service.

Many years later, I was able to take the experiences that had transformed me and apply them to help transform a college. My 18-year journey at Elon College, now Elon University, gave me the assurance that planning intensively with a dedicated team of people could change a *good* college into a *thriving* and *excellent* college. Being actively engaged in student life, admissions, the Elon Experiences, and advancement involved me in Elon's comprehensive development and growth at an important time in its history.

I know that my experience on the leadership team at Elon was a matter of being in the right place at the right time, and what a time it was! What a privilege to be part of a team with a board of trustees that decided early to put students at the center of everything. Before anyone was talking about engaged and experiential learning, Elon was devoted to making it happen, and planned for it. Before anyone was worrying about discount rates and how they would affect the future of higher education, faculty and staff at Elon knew that value proposition was more important than money and scholarships in the college choice.

As the college grew, and quality and student engagement became integral to every program and department, I came to expect that anything was possible. Now, Elon University stands proudly with national visibility. Elon is a significant university that has all of the attributes of excellence and continues to thrive!

My personal growth and professional experience at these two special schools nurtured my passion for the value of small private colleges and universities. This passion compelled me to become a founding partner and owner of Credo, a comprehensive consulting firm dedicated to small private colleges, and has led me with great conviction to the writing of this book.

My work in partnership with more than 200 private colleges over the last 15 years led me to think carefully and intentionally about the elements present in those that were *thriving* and absent in those only *surviving*. At Credo, we decided years ago to offer a no-fee Strategy Day to private college presidents, a day to focus on their agendas, issues, and aspirations. We asked, "What keeps you up at night?" More and more presidents accepted our invitation, and their thoughts and experiences began to accumulate.

After hundreds of these days, we began to see patterns, and started to intentionally identify the elements that were making a difference in whether a college was surviving, thriving, or balancing somewhere in between. Those elements became clear enough that we began to speak about them externally. We were privileged to present the Thriving College Framework at both the Council of Independent Colleges Presidents Institute and the National Association of Independent Colleges and Universities Annual Meeting. The nine elements that Credo and I have examined and refined provide the framework for the chapters of this book. The elements are closely interrelated. This speaks to the interplay between the areas of a thriving college, and the level of connection needed to make all the elements work in concert.

Because so much of what is in this book comes from my own intuition and conversations with these presidents over the last fifteen years, it is written in the first person. After the outline for the book was complete, I began to see that current research was lining up with many of our own findings. At that time, I asked Dr. Rick

Mann if he would join me in authoring the book. Rick has taken on the responsibility of accumulating the research and readings that substantiate and set into context our findings. I appreciate the depth this has given to the practicality of our daily work.

Dr. Rick Mann

It didn't take long after I became a new college president in 2005 to know that I needed a Strategy Day with Credo and Joanne Soliday. It was an opportunity to sit with a veteran and talk through what was keeping me awake at night. That began a wonderful journey with Joanne and Credo that continues to this day. We share a common passion for private higher education, and a common vision for thriving institutions.

My experience in higher education began with large public institutions, both as a student and as a professional. When I joined my first small private institution as the vice president for academic affairs and provost, I was immediately struck by how rich the experience was for students compared to my public university experience. The level of engagement by students, faculty, and staff was remarkable.

In 2012, two significant events happened in my life and leadership. First, my wife, Cheri, was continuing to face some health issues that were not well-suited for the cold climate of Minnesota, so I decided not to seek another term as president of Crown College (MN), and began looking for opportunities in a warmer climate. Second, a sabbatical in my last year at Crown gave me invaluable space to research the applications of a balanced scorecard to private colleges and universities.

Over the previous five years, I had gained valuable experience with the balanced scorecard at our institution, but it was our accreditation process with the Higher Learning Commission of the North Central Association that moved my focus forward. They emphasized that the balanced scorecard had been so transformational in our strategic planning evolution that we should look at sharing this with other institutions. Working with a half-dozen institutions over the 2012-2013 academic year convinced me that there was a growing convergence for institutions between accreditation, strategy, and disruptive environments that made the balanced scorecard an ideal fit for this season in higher education. My interest in this type of strategic planning and assessment led me to a position as professor of leadership and strategy at Trevecca Nazarene University. I also developed a consulting partnership with Credo with a focus on strategy, strategic planning, and applications of a balanced scorecard to private colleges and universities.

In the midst of our work, I often heard Joanne talk about her desire to write a book around the Thriving College Framework developed by Credo, and sharing with others her experience in dealing with numerous small private colleges. I was intrigued by her idea. I had written other books and served as a journal managing editor, so we talked in some detail about how together we could balance the art and science of higher education leadership. Some of you may be familiar with Max De Pree's famous treatise, "Leadership is an Art" (1989). Joanne's "art" – her vast experience with private college presidents, boards, and campus leaders – is shared throughout the book. If you know Joanne, those sections of the book are obvious: full of conviction, insight, and passion. I've offered herein some "science" – a brief analysis of recent research on the topics addressed.

It has been a joy to partner with Joanne on this project. Her passion is contagious, and I am convinced that what Joanne is sharing is crucial in helping institutions move from surviving to thriving. I also believe that the research provides a complementary lens to the topics addressed by Joanne.

Rick and I originally began building lists of suggested readings for this book, but every time I talked to a president, I heard something about a good book that was making a difference in his or her personal motivation. It seemed to make sense to ask presidents directly what books they were finding useful in their leadership – so we did! At the end of the book, you'll find a section on *What Presidents are Reading*, and many of you have given us your input. I think you will find value in this section, and maybe a few more books for your reading list.

My commitment to giving leaders the tools that will make a difference in helping their colleges and universities thrive has never been stronger. It is my intention that this book be used to assist college and university leadership teams in their planning. It is designed to bring forward some of the crucial variables to consider.

At the end of each chapter there are discussion questions for use at retreats and in strategic settings. Credo's Thriving Framework Inventory, a companion online survey, has been developed to accompany this book to assist leadership teams in understanding where particular areas of urgency exist on their campuses, and set benchmark data to gauge future growth and improvement. You can find more information on the survey at the close of the book.

At Credo, one of our company values is to have a servant's heart. It is with a servant's heart that I offer these thoughts based on many years of experience and privilege. I hope you will feel the passion and optimism behind this book, and that my tale of two colleges and the 200 that followed will be of assistance to you. We know without a doubt that private colleges *must* be an option! There are too many of us with potential who need them.

The Thriving
College Framework

Courageous &
Collaborative
Leadership

Vision

Institutional
Self-Esteem

Institutional
Story

Habit of Reflection
& Intentionality

Culture of
Planning &
Innovation

Net Revenue
& Strategic
Finance

Student Learning
& Success

Transformative
Environments

Chapter 2

Courageous & Collaborative Leadership

Cabinet meetings were clearly dysfunctional. Everyone knew that one person in the room was changing the dynamic. It was clear that it affected every discussion and every process. There were side discussions after the primary meetings, and much of the conversation between vice presidents was about how dysfunctional the meetings and the person were. This cabinet member had been at the institution for more than 20 years, and had many community connections. Any action taken to terminate her appointment would have been difficult and heart-wrenching. But ignoring the situation threatened to immobilize the mission of the institution.

The situation above is not unusual. Every president comes upon the dilemma – or the opportunity – of having a vice-presidential team member who is not functioning at the highest levels. There are many other decisions like the one above that are difficult, but affect the welfare of the institution profoundly. These decisions are made by each president dependent upon the ability to balance *attention to institutional success* and *attention to constituency approval.* Strategy, credentials, intellect, and communication skills will determine the value of the position of president, but I will always believe that the ability to balance people and tasks in decision-making will be at the center of success and courageous leadership.

As I look back over a long career in higher education, some crucial areas of successful leadership emerge in relation to leadership teams, the role of the board of trustees, and the courage of strong leaders to stay.

People

CABINET ISSUES: I'VE GOT YOUR BACK

On a weekly basis, a president or board member will ask me what the most essential ingredient is for a sustainable thriving college. That question has never been difficult for me to answer. The most important element to the health of an institution in today's urgent times is a strong and capable leadership team. Several studies highlight the difference effective leaders and teams make. Kotter's research describes most organizations as "over-managed and underled" (1990, p. 85). Appointing an effective leadership team or president's cabinet, however, is only half of the battle – the best teams are clearly collaborative (Ibarra & Hansen, 2011). To survive in the atmosphere that faces us in higher education today, every leadership team must have each other's backs – trust! – and must be able to play in each other's sandboxes – integration!

Tasks

Trust

Trust among the members of the president's cabinet demands a whole new level of leadership development, and is one of the most important requirements in the functioning of a team (Lencioni, 2012). The agenda of one team member can frequently become more important than the strategic agenda of the institution, and has the potential to derail success. I am frequently working with a college cabinet and I become absolutely sure that there is an elephant in the room! That elephant is usually the personality, capability, and entitlement of a vice president who is not playing by the same rules. Courageous leadership here would demand that the issue be addressed, but confrontation skills are not in everyone's portfolio. Richard Hackman, Harvard professor of organizational psychology and expert on teams, recommends that teams invite in an outside coach to help them grow in their effectiveness (Coutu, 2009).

Even external coaching doesn't mean that cohesiveness will happen overnight. Team traction will take time to develop. Hackman emphasizes that teams need to be real and authentic by spending adequate time together (Coutu, 2009). Higher levels of trust relate to higher levels of team performance, and also have enormously positive effects on long-term teams versus short-term teams (De Jong & Elfring, 2010).

Cabinet Meetings

Meetings that do not start on time, don't have a clear agenda, and don't have clear decision-making points are not in the best interest of the institution as a whole, and will continue to frustrate members of the cabinet. When a meeting consists primarily of urgent operational details, it distracts teams from a clear focus on pre-determined strategies. In Lencioni's "Death By Meeting" (2004), he highlights how meetings should be reframed at the visionary, strategic, and tactical levels. For example, a team could have a visionary meeting each quarter, a strategy meeting each month, and a tactical meeting each week. It's a joy for me to watch a weekly cabinet meeting when agendas are clear and the room is unmistakably energized. They set the stage for the whole week, ensure relevant topics are being addressed, and reinforce with vice presidents that strategy is leading the way. It is a missed opportunity to use them in any other way, and a step in courageous leadership to be coached to lead them effectively.

Integration – Come Play in My Sandbox!

The days of planning for the *big five* are over! Silos are out! Finance/administration, fundraising, student affairs, academic affairs, and enrollment can no longer function without absolute integration with each other. I think it's safe to say that they *never* should have

> The value proposition needed for parents to pay the cost of a private college education is completely linked to our ability to see student learning as a comprehensive process.

functioned like that. It takes a courageous leader to break up these long-protected traditions. The value proposition needed for parents to pay the cost of a private college education is completely linked to our ability to see student learning as a comprehensive process. We must attend to these areas with the big picture in our heads. Learning takes place when a student is settling financial accounts, getting along with his or her roommate, using technology, working on a project, sitting on a bench with a professor looking at beautiful green grass, and having a conversation. It is all integrated. This is achieved when divisions and departments are less integrated by organizational charts and more integrated around the student experience (Kvavik & Handburg, 2000). The senior team must function with fewer silos to make it work (Katz, 2010; Lencioni, 2006). It is much easier for presidents to attend individually to each of the areas in the big five. It takes courage to proclaim that their integration is essential, and measure that integration with appropriate metrics.

PRESIDENTS WHO STAY

When we talk about sustainable and courageous leadership in small private colleges and universities, it is impossible to ignore current trends. We are seeing more and more presidents from nontraditional backgrounds, and presidential rotations are more frequent. Song & Hartley (2012) report that the average length of presidential tenure at CIC member institutions dropped 17% from 8.5 years in 2006 to 7.1 years in 2011. While the tenure is getting shorter, the same researchers report that 86% of CIC presidents are very satisfied with their jobs, which is higher than their public institutional counterparts.

As I study presidents who stay with institutions for longer terms, it has become evident to me that they generally move through four distinct phases in order to stay energized, committed, challenged, and fulfilled. This takes courage! It means there is an element of self-reflection and awareness that is a gift to the college.

Phase One: Operational

New presidents feel most unprepared in the areas of fundraising, legal issues, financial/capital issues, and entrepreneurial endeavors

(Hartley & Godin, 2009). However, coming into the role, there is a need to understand the workings of all programs and departments, to get arms around anything related to enrollment (thankfully!). There is also a need to become acquainted with the people in the campus community, so presidents in this phase are highly visible. New presidents also have a great interest in understanding the effect processes and systems have on the future of the institution. It is an essential phase, and can be draining or replenishing based on the personality of the president. Some can't come out of this phase, and others can't wait to get out! But they must move forward. The other phases are too important to their future.

Phase Two: Campus Leadership Development

At this time in a college presidency, the president's cabinet or leadership team is generally becoming more permanent. The players have been chosen and/or embraced by the president, and they are now beginning to function in their roles with a great deal of trust and integration. In Phase Two presidencies, I can really begin to see delegation reach higher levels. The president is beginning to take his or her hands off the steering wheel so vice presidents can drive the operations, and the vice presidents are delegating work to their teams with confidence.

It is essential for all presidents to be sure that his or her vice presidents have a trusted second-chair staff member who will back them up in all instances. The burnout rate for vice presidents at small private colleges is sky-high. They function strategically, but then go back and do the implementation themselves because attention has not been paid to that crucial number-two position. Many don't have it, and others have someone in it that cannot replace them. In order for a successful college president to begin looking ahead to the next phase, leadership development at this level is critical.

Phase Three: External Relations

Now it is time to go beyond the campus and focus on fundraising! While donors have been cultivated all along and relationships have been built, the simple asks are ending, and the more complicated and transformational gift period has begun. Presidents in this phase have to reach deeper into understanding family relationships and businesses. Proposals and gift possibilities are at a whole new level and demand focused attention. Community relationships become crucially important. Land acquisition and zoning issues are now safe to discuss because stability is evident. It is clearly a phase when external relationships have taken priority, and operations, programs, and planning are being done through the leadership of strong vice presidents. Board members begin to expect big things here.

I am sad to say that during this phase, I see the most doubt creeping in. It comes from all angles. The honeymoon is over – board members, faculty, and staff are watching and wondering what's next. It is right about now that every president begins to be identified for the major strength or contribution that will shape his or her presidential legacy. In this phase, I hear conversations about *enrollment presidents* or *student presidents*. You can be sure that whatever the president *did* do, it is now time for fundraising! This is also a time when presidents begin to wonder if it would be better to move on. The most courageous leadership happens when they have the ability to move into Phase Four with confidence, success, and humility.

Phase Four: Partnerships and Significance

It took me a long time to identify this one. I could see it happening and knew it was a stage of the most ultimate commitment and investment, but I had to ask many questions and hear a broad spectrum of stories to see it more clearly. I have used the word significance for several reasons. When things are humming along nicely, key indicators are exciting, and the presidency has reached beyond the 10-year mark, boredom can set in. The decision to stay depends upon the ability of the institution and the president to design something that is significant and meaningful for the future.

> The decision to stay depends upon the ability of the institution and the president to design something that is significant and meaningful for the future.

I have seen many presidents develop partnerships abroad that recapture the initial sparkle of mission (Fielden, 2010). Healthcare programs with hospitals, community development projects, book initiatives, teaching in national forums, and other major projects represent the formation of partnerships that allow personal significance for the longer journey.

Assisting presidents in making longer-term commitments is a charge I wish boards of trustees would take more seriously. The changes that occur when presidents rotate frequently slow progress and sometimes change vision abruptly. Stability in leadership is crucial in the current climate of higher education.

Turn-Around Presidents

Of course, the phases are not as black and white when we are looking right at them, and they often blend and integrate into each other. The one clear exception I see is the obvious appointment of a turn-around president. Turn-around presidents look different to me. They stay five to seven years, clearly LOVE the operational and building stage, and they are good at it!

There are some turn-around presidents who have been invaluable to the history of small private colleges, but they have been careful. The successful ones have paid attention to the following things:

1. They are sure that the board owns the vision for the future, and that it will continue to strengthen after they leave.
2. They leverage the current crisis situation of the college for good, and use it to implement much-needed changes in culture and practice.
3. They are careful not to raise the enrollment of the institution by raising the discount rate sky-high, then leaving that problem for leaders of the future.
4. They are careful not to enroll a larger quantity of students who are not best-fit for the institution. Bringing the enrollment up by continually recruiting large classes of students and driving retention figures down is not a stable way to ensure the future.

I am impressed with turn-around presidents and their ability to jump-start a new future for a surviving college, but not if their own personal motivation is to quickly make good news and leave a bad foundation in place for the future.

BOARD MEMBERS: ENGAGED AND STRATEGIC

The tendency to panic over financial and enrollment issues has put too many board members into what I would classify as micro-managing roles. Those of us who consult in colleges these days are noticing something that we did not notice years ago: The tendency of board members to wander *out of their seats*, or away from their primary areas of focus, and often with good reason! I believe most board members would *love* to be *in* their seats, but they must be comfortable there. Effective governing boards are an invaluable asset to the health and strength of a college or university. Research done by the Association of Governing Boards of Universities and Colleges (2012a) reflects the best practices of today's board. Some of these include focusing on the oversight of the president, engagement in strategic planning, and ensuring the accomplishment of the institutional mission. In more recent years, boards have been pressed even more to deal with rising costs in higher education (AGB Press, 2012b). It will take bold and courageous leadership for our presidents and boards to design their unique roles and responsibilities with integrity. A board must be confident in a president's ability to lead, and a president must be confident that board members (and especially the board chair) will stand in support.

Engagement

An engaging, significant board meeting is *not* a three-hour, one-way report. Presidents must recruit board members who possess the ability to help propel their colleges and universities to another level. Once they accept those seats, board members must be given the opportunity to offer the wisdom and insight for which they were appointed. With better planning, your board members will know they play a significant role in the mission, and that will sustain their enthusiasm. Board members want to be involved at the strategic level and be less tactical, especially when it comes to finance (Fain, 2009).

Presidents often ask me why their board members are not more philanthropic. The capacity for giving is there, but the willingness is not. Board engagement is directly linked to fundraising. We will address it in *Net Revenue and Strategic Finance*, but I am amazed at how many of our administrative teams do not engage boards in activities that will capture their hearts. It is wonderful to watch engaging board meetings where you have a clear expectation that because of what has just been shared, there will surely be a gift forthcoming to propel an initiative forward. We have the responsibility to bring philanthropy to the forefront because we have done something that compels it.

It is much easier to *lead* a board meeting than to *facilitate* one. Presidents need to facilitate board meetings effectively and need to train their board chairs to do the same. The strategic future of each institution depends upon it.

Strategic Planning

There is often confusion in leadership around the issue of strategic planning for an institution. Let us be clear that the board of trustees is responsible for the oversight, not the execution, of the strategic plan. In today's best practices, boards provide headlights, or direction, and delegate the nuts and bolts of the planning to the president of the college (Bryson, 2011; Carver, 2006). We have written much more about this in *Culture of Planning and Innovation*, but it is relevant here because of the courage it takes to clarify and communicate appropriate roles. Many trustee members have been on various boards with different functioning philosophies. Some come with the expectation that they will actually do the planning for the institution, and then assist in the implementation. Others are used to running their own companies this way, and without clear direction, they will feel compelled to assist in that same manner.

Committees

It has been an honor and a pleasure to watch board committees functioning in a healthy and helpful way. It has also been discouraging to watch them when they inhibit progress because they have not been guided to contribute at appropriate levels. Vice presidents should be excited and energized to do some truly strategic work with their committees. Committee chairs should be excited and energized to be ambassadors to the board around those strategic initiatives.

What a joy to hear enrollment committee participants explain this year's funnel, or see the advancement committee chair take on the role of moving the $1,000 donor number to a new high! Boards do their best work when relationships are strong and learning communities are developed within the context of the board and its committees (Shields, 2007), but leadership here has to be courageous. By courageous, I don't mean telling board committee chairs what to do. It takes the utmost skill to place the right agenda, the right script, and the right objectives in the hands of a board committee chair. This kind of courageous, collaborative, and innovative leadership can make or break a board meeting issue and vote at the main board session.

COLLABORATION AND URGENCY: DECIDE ALREADY!

Earlier in the chapter, I mention the need for balance in decision making. I also said that it would be crucial to the future of stability in higher education for presidents to understand how important that balance is. Many authors are writing about the need for decision making and strategy in higher education to be different, because the times are different (Alfred, 2006). We simply cannot take the time we used to take to do the things we used to do! The need for these teams to function at a high level could not be greater (Fullan & Scott, 2009). Components of this effectiveness include decision making, pacing, and collaboration (Alfred,

> Today's leaders and teams need to find a balance of clarity, leadership, collaboration, and individual accountability.

2006). For important collaborative decisions to be made at a higher pace, communication becomes key (Kotter, 2007). Presidents have to understand what collaboration means in their culture and combine it with best-practice decision making in urgent situations. Likewise, moving from strategy to execution is key in realizing institutional outcomes (Kaplan and Norton, 2008). The process still needs to be clear and informative, but must dictate a decision-making point in time. There is an art and science to this process of decision making. When comparing leader-directed teams to empowered teams, Lorinkova, Pearsall, and Sims (2013) demonstrate that in the short run, leader-directed teams out-perform empowered teams. However, over time, empowered teams overtake the effectiveness of leader-directed teams. Today's leaders and teams need to find a balance of clarity, leadership, collaboration, and individual accountability.

Roles and Responsibilities

Clarity on campuses about who makes which decisions is essential. When it is clear which level of decisions would benefit from *information* and which from *collaboration*, we will have less stress in our college and university systems. The Carver Model clarifies who has responsibility for what (Carver, 2006). His process allows boards and senior teams to define the parameters and boundaries for decision making. For example, the board of trustees authorizes the faculty to make all curricular decisions as long as they comply with state standards.

Communication

Over the last 15 years, I have been privileged to facilitate over 100 strategic planning processes. In *every single instance* – every one! – the number one internal threat to the institution has been identified as internal communication. It is clear that we, as educators, place a high priority on it, but it is also clear that endless discussion about decisions made in the past will not serve us well today.

Communication is the simple key to almost everything we need to solve in the campus environment. It's not about talking, but about deciding who needs to know what when and making sure attention is being paid to those needs. Ineffective communication leads to time wasted, and clear communication diminishes distraction and allows us to focus on what is most important. When cabinet members communicate well with one another, the whole organization benefits (Kotter, 2012).

Urgency

It is distressing to see how many simple decisions do not get made in our colleges and universities today. So much is tabled and neglected because of a perceived lack of urgency, only to rise again with more complications and potential for distraction. I resist words like *turnaround* and *crisis*, but embrace the word *urgency* in thinking about what we need to do to help small private colleges thrive. There is probably less to turn around and more to clear up! Kotter (2008) refers to this as a true sense of urgency, which avoids complacency on the one hand and false urgency on the other. If systems and processes are clean, and decision-making is quick and clear, a number of roadblocks disappear.

Trust – Again!

The careful balancing act between collaboration and urgency is built on a foundation of trust. When leadership has been transparent and clear, it is much easier to move through the journey of difficult and efficient decision making.

I am continually struck by the positive reactions from faculty and staff to decisions that are made based on a financial model, or good data and research. They respond beautifully to solid indicators, and it gives them the evidence they need to trust the administrative direction. But too frequently, decisions are made without this important base of information. Mistrust develops, and a culture emerges that is difficult to manage.

THE RIGHT PEOPLE IN THE RIGHT PLACES

There is absolutely no way to put the right people in the right places in our institutions without courageous leadership. Institutions have struggled through human resource nightmares for decades and continue to do so because of our consistent lack of best practice performance evaluations, communication skills, and an ability to assess skill sets in the areas crucial to success.

Performance Evaluations

I am amazed by the differences in performance evaluations. The range of quality in their substance is detrimental to our future as educators. We collect data from others about performance and satisfaction, but don't use it strategically to make corrections. We fail to put in writing specific goals and solutions that can bring people to their highest potential. Lencioni (2007) reminds us that when we lack organizational or role clarity, our colleagues are not at their best. If we do manage to put those goals in writing, we still struggle to communicate them effectively so that the individual on the receiving end sees that roadmap as helpful and not critical. Our tendency is to bring up weaknesses and not emphasize strengths, and we are often not committed to putting the right professional development in place to solve the problems. Recent clear and compelling research points to the ability of adult professionals to grow and change (Ibarra & Hansen, 2011). Halvorson (2011) makes the point that one of the most self-defeating behaviors is the notion that we are born with certain qualities and others can't be learned.

> We collect data from others about performance and satisfaction, but don't use it strategically to make corrections.

While there is a slow movement toward merit pay, we also struggle philosophically with the issue, and subsequently are not able to incentivize those activities and qualities that bring the most success to our mission. It is important for each college or university to place a priority on best-practice tools for this purpose.

Strengthening the Middle

At every institution I am tempted to gather up the strong, loyal director-level staff that make all of the wheels turn, give them a better view of the bigger picture, and help them understand their role in making institutional goals a success. They should be respected, consulted, and empowered to be the next generation of leaders. You could name these individuals at your institution. It's the person who year after year has taken care of all of the details of graduation, or the person who continues to make orientation smooth and effective. Oftentimes, it is a registrar, a director of student success, a director of career development, a director of residence life, the supervisor of the maintenance crew, or a star instructor. We often wonder what we would do without these people, but they are the last people to whom we offer professional development and the last people we reward and appreciate. They seldom know the big picture, and often wonder why some of the tasks that they do are important. This group at the middle of our mission is crucial to our future. Intentional placement of key leaders can build a strong future through effective succession planning (Rothwell, 2010). I applaud colleges and universities who are identifying them, developing them, and delegating larger responsibilities to them.

EMBRACING INNOVATION

The need for innovation and change will grow in importance more than we know over these next years. There is an absolute need to do things differently. A lack of willingness to change can represent a major obstacle to courageous and collaborative leadership, and long-standing organizations like colleges and universities struggle with staying engaged in innovation. Research has shown that the best organizations are those that are committed to historical rootedness in the organization's core values, while at the same time actively pursuing innovation (Collins & Porras, 1994). There are a few key issues, though, that can hold leaders back.

Fear

Because so much has been changing in higher education, each institution has inherited a special group of gatekeepers. The motivation of this group of faculty, and sometimes staff, is pure. They believe that they are here to protect the liberal arts and in every direction they look, there is a threat. Somehow, we must address the need for change and communicate our devotion to the central goals of liberal arts education at the same time.

Inefficient Processes

It is difficult to change things when we don't know how! Changes in how we schedule, teach, and provide services demand careful re-thinking. Never have I seen more need for process-mapping systems so they will be student-centered and not faculty- and staff-centered. In business, they might call all of this re-engineering. The knowledge we actually need is closer than we think. We just have to map it.

Lack of Urgency

We are so used to conversation and discussion being central to everything that we do. It is a loss to think that we might not be able to thoroughly vet and discuss all issues, at all levels, at all times. We were used to that, and we miss the debate! But the urgency of the environment in which we find ourselves demands clearer and more concise paths. We must change our culture, and that is difficult. And although we want to protect ourselves from the constant press for productivity all around us, we must find quicker and more fulfilling ways to innovate and change.

Data Gaps

We will address the need for data in great detail in the *Habit of Reflection and Intentionality* chapter. It is important to note here that much of our hesitancy to innovate and change comes from a lack of research-driven knowledge that would help give us comfort. It is dangerous in these times to make good decisions and innovative changes when we don't have the data. We need to be anchored in information that we trust!

SUMMARY

There is no doubt about it – this chapter is about people! It is about how we treat them, how we inform them, how we identify their strengths, and how we nurture the seeds of significance. From the members of the board of trustees to the president, from the faculty to the administrative staff of the institution, the future lies in identifying significant roles for good people and applauding their achievement. Without this, we will not be able to move forward. The very best strategies we can develop will be useless without the right implementers and motivators.

DISCUSSION QUESTIONS:
COURAGEOUS & COLLABORATIVE LEADERSHIP

- Are the president and the members of the cabinet engaged in leadership development?
- Is there a spirit of innovation on the president's cabinet?
- Are the president and the cabinet engaged in self-evaluation annually?
- Does the cabinet function collaboratively as a team?
- Do the members of the cabinet trust each other?
- Are there too many times when one cabinet member's decision impacts another area of the campus without prior communication?
- Do the members of the cabinet feel empowered to make decisions in their areas?
- Are there unaddressed deficits in skill, knowledge, or experience at the cabinet level?
- Is there more than a normal amount of tension between the administration and the faculty of the institution?
- Are problems at the institution being addressed and solutions implemented in a timely manner?
- Does each vice president at the institution have a strong back-up person on his/her team?
- Are decisions at the institution communicated in a clear and consistent way?
- Is the decision-making process at the institution clear and transparent?
- Are there any areas of the institution that are being capped (unable to reach highest potential) by one individual?

- Are there entitlements in place at the institution that inhibit innovation?
- Do you perceive that the board of trustees at the institution is micro-managing?
- Is there a process in place for self-assessment and development of the board?
- Are the committees of the board functioning effectively?
- Is the board of trustees actively engaged during their meetings?
- What are the obstacles to change and innovation that you encounter?
- How have those obstacles been addressed?

Chapter 3

Vision

In preparation for a strategic planning project at a small private college, I asked the president to bring me a copy of any documents that might help us determine vision for the next three to five years. When she delivered the documents to me, I was not surprised. There were 10! There were two copies of a mission statement. One statement had been developed by a self-appointed group feeling the need for a mission statement update. That document had never been voted upon. The second was the mission statement that was printed in the college catalog. A third document was a set of goals that had been developed several years ago by a planning group. The goals were not part of the strategic plan. They were reflective of what that group believed the college culture should be like. There was also a document with core values listed. There was another document stating the objectives for the new general education core. There were two vision statements, each designed by past presidents. There was an old strategic plan with a list of imperatives. And finally, there were positioning statements written by marketing consultants.

I have learned to always ask for the accumulation of these documents before beginning to work on the new strategic plan! Each of them means something to someone, but you can imagine the confusion among the campus community about the direction for the future.

The story above begs us to examine what our institutions really need to provide intentional forward movement. No directional statement will be compelling if it is not clear and relevant. I believe we really only need three specific guides in order to plan well and execute appropriately. These guides come in the form of a *mission statement*, a *vision statement*, and a set of *core values*. With these guides, we are able to have direction and passion to do what we love to do.

If you read much on mission, vision, and values, there are lots of variations on what these three words mean (Mrozinki, 2010). As we go through this material, we are using the following simple definitions:

- Mission: A statement of **what you do**, the purpose you serve. The mission is often focused around an unmet need in higher education.
- Values: Values are **why you do what you do**. Values are foundational, support the mission, and provide principles that guide your work.
- Vision: A statement on **where you are going**. Vision gives you a clear and preferred picture of an aspirational future, the desired experience at your institution. Vision has its foundation in mission, is informed by values and positioning, and provides direction.

MISSION: THE PURPOSE

Meacham asks, "What's the use of a mission statement?" (2008). A carefully constructed mission statement is written because it is important for every college or university to project to all of its constituencies what they do. We have all seen mission statements that are a full page and some that are two sentences long. But it is fair to say that most are laden with language that is accumulated from traditions and historical information that everyone is afraid to adjust. Virtually all colleges and universities have mission statements that form the foundation of their quality and improvement work (O'Hearn, 2004). Strong mission statements have also been shown to increase organizational effectiveness (Cady, Wheeler, DeWolf, & Brodke, 2011).

Mission statements of the future will need to be highly relevant and solidly foundational in order to be effective. The words themselves should evoke emotion and commitment. Every member of the campus community should be able to read the mission statement and know that they are in the right place at the right time to do something special. The statement is the reason why the college or university exists. There is no more appropriate time in the history of higher education than now to make an effort to clarify what we do and the difference it will make in students' lives.

Plan First, Mission Second!

It is almost impossible to develop a mission statement in today's environment using the same philosophy we have used in the past. Common practice has been to develop this statement and then begin to plan based on what we have written, but universities are entities on the move, and our constituencies expect more from us than ever – we cannot develop our mission statements in a vacuum. The basics of how we learn have changed so much that we are compelled to address the needs of students today in very different ways. If we are not careful, our mission statement can inhibit us from the innovative thinking we need to do in order to make a difference to the traditional and nontraditional students of this era.

In this atmosphere of rapid movement, I recommend that mission statements be reviewed *after* strategic planning exercises take place. The exercise of scanning our environment and understanding our students completely is an important thing to accomplish before we redesign a description of mission. That isn't to say that the roots of our colleges and universities are not integral to the process, but it's entirely possible that creating these foundational statements without clear knowledge of current realities can prohibit us from the innovation necessary to thrive in higher education today.

> Creating foundational statements without clear knowledge of current realities can prohibit us from the innovation necessary to thrive.

So How Does it Happen?

I have examined many methods for the revision of mission statements, and I find no substitute for the deliberation of three or four strategic and committed individuals who are assigned to the task. A careful review of the insights, research, and strategic thinking during the planning process will provide the necessary insight for this deliberation.

The process can be very smooth when this group of respected individuals presents the elements of a new or refined mission statement to faculty, the president's cabinet and the board of trustees for their review. After the elements are agreed upon, the word-smithing is not as challenging. I have watched this process be enormously difficult when everyone is trying to choose the right words. Choosing the elements makes for an easier beginning. The words can be stitched together easily when agreement on the elements is reached.

How Often?

Mission statements don't change very much! In fact, you may see only one revision or change during your years of tenure at a college or university. Some mission statements have been set in stone for more than 50 years. It is not something we want to do often, but when changes in our field push us in new directions, every college or university should be looking at their mission statement to be sure that its elements continue to be relevant and embraced.

VISION: THE DIRECTION

The vision statement is fuel for the journey! It is what drives us. It is the inspiration that brings the mission to life on our campuses, and it is memorable. It brings clarity to our aspirational future when we are in desperate need of clarity and significance. Every college needs a good vision statement, and needs it now.

When we have a clear mission statement that says what we do, then the vision statement is a portrayal of how we will live that out over the next ten years. I wish I had $10 for every time a president has asked me how to begin to write a vision statement. One research study states that 80% of institutions have changed their vision statement in the last decade (Abelman & Dalessandro, 2009). It does seem that presidents understand that this duty is a major part of their role. I find that the most difficult issue for presidents to address is in the difference between writing a *vision* and writing a *vision statement*. Most of the time they are able to write two or three pages about the future and how it might look. The difficulty is in taking those thoughts and bringing them to life in one or two sentences that are concise and compelling enough to motivate an institution.

The Default Vision

Even though many experts write and talk incessantly about the need for vision to be compelling and motivating, I often find that there is a default vision operating in many of our colleges and universities: balancing the budget. On campuses with this default vision, the bottom line is driving every decision and shaping the culture of the campus community. When a college or university is in survival mode, living basically by watching the fall enrollment number all the way until September 15th, vision has been co-opted by a preoccupation with net revenue. If you don't believe me, just read the *Inside Higher Ed* 2011 Survey of College Presidents (Green). Of the approximately 1,000 presidents who responded, almost half (49%) of all presidents surveyed said that the most important issue confronting their institutions was budget shortfall.

In this book, we are very conscious about net revenue. It is one of the nine elements we believe must be in clear focus in order to be a thriving college. There will clearly be no mission accomplished without a good revenue margin, but a total dependence on one fall number is not indicative of good planning, and clearly overshadows any aspirational, future-focused vision statement.

It's a Connection Tool!

There must be integration and connection present to thrive! Having a compelling vision means that it connects everything that is being initiated and accomplished. It means that watching a final number is not nearly as healthy as watching the leading indicators that predict it and make it possible. It means that the processes and functions in one office or department are not nearly as important as the overarching decisions connected to the vision statement.

> Our tendency to function in silos is dangerous to the health of the learning we value.

Our tendency to function in silos is dangerous to the health of the learning we value. The vision statement should pull it all together and keep us focused. It should connect us to each other and to our strategic plan so that there is no question about how we move forward. There should be no new initiatives that do not relate directly to vision. Projects outside the vision distract from and dilute our connections.

I have seen this distraction again and again in performing arts center projects across the country. Before every musician and artist scrambles to critique this comment, let me explain that I love those performing arts centers! There is, of course, incredible value in being the center of culture in small towns across America. I would even go as far as to say that we, as educators, have a responsibility to make this happen. However, when this expensive endeavor comes about as a reflection of one president or donor's dream, and the vision for the future has already been cast with the need for funding in other areas, the connection is lost and the campus community is confused. I continue to see beautiful performing arts centers without the robust focus on core programming necessary to reach highest potential. It is because they were not connected to the vision for the future, and the strategic initiatives have not been put in place to make them come alive! Our goal is alignment of mission, vision, and values with strategic priorities, objectives, and measures.

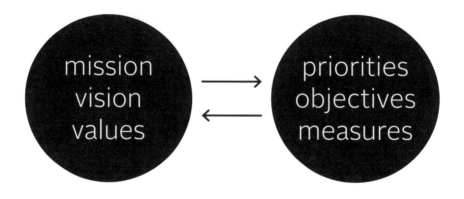

VALUES: THE CORE

Over the years, I have heard more and more conversation about how we go about accomplishing our mission and vision. Many faculty and staff members are experiencing a substantial amount of change in the way things have always been done. Because these changes are essential to keep pace with the new normal, there is a greater need to talk about how we will live together in a community and serve the students of the future. It is at this juncture that recognizing an institution's core values becomes key.

I often think that if the refinement of the mission and vision statements are at hand, the easy way to start is with a discussion about core values (Hill, 2013). There's great comfort to be found in stating values. It helps us all to remember why we do what we do and why integrity on our journey is so important (Lencioni, 2002).

I love watching teams examine values. The discussion is often cleaner than the ones about mission and vision, and tends to bring unity. It is a place where most people agree, creating a launching pad for a small, focused team to move on to the more difficult tasks of fleshing out mission and vision.

Just as brevity is important when crafting a vision statement, concise language is key when articulating values. Lencioni says, "When leaders who adopt too many values finally realize what they've done and that there is no hope for actually putting their many values to practical use, they often end up ignoring them altogether" (2012, p. 92). It's also harder to get buy-in from the greater campus community when values are too lengthy. Three to five refined values that fully represent why that institution does what it does generally allow for the most impact. When a member of the campus community can tell me what the values are, I know they are memorable, and have the ability to stay at the forefront of decisions and actions across campus.

WHO OWNS ALL THIS?

The more frequent turnover of presidents has been troubling for me to watch. Although we discuss this in the chapter on courageous leadership, the impact of turnover on mission, vision, and values is unmistakable, and bears mention here.

Inconsistency in leadership takes a toll on an institution, and this area is particularly vulnerable. I have seen some colleges change vision two to three times in a 10-year period. The dramatic decline of health during these times can be devastating. When vision is entirely owned by the college president, there is a distinct risk that a presidential change will cause all nine elements in the framework to falter from lack of direction.

It is for these reasons that the board of trustees must own the mission and vision for the future and protect it during presidential change. The Association of Governing Boards of Universities and Colleges "Effective Governing Boards" guide lists the number one responsibility of the board as, "Establish, disseminate, and keep current the institution's mission" (2007). That does not mean that a new president should hesitate to be inspirational and compelling about the future. It also doesn't mean that a new president can't embrace a new vision statement, but it does mean that someone needs to carefully assess the implications for the long-term health of the college, and ensure campus community buy-in and ownership.

I've seen the turnover problem play out in one particular scenario more than once. Say one president believes that adult education should be a part of the future of the institution. The next president sees it as a threat to the liberal arts, and either ignores it or begins to eliminate it. Revenue changes dramatically, but the new philosophy is embraced and acted upon. A couple of years later, the dilemma of decreased net revenue is evident, the board becomes concerned, and a whole new layer of problems rise to the surface. Questions about significant changes to vision should be addressed at the outset, before major shifts are underway, to ensure the stability of values, mission, and ultimately, the institution.

GET HELP!

Talking about how important the vision statement is to the future is a good start, but writing it is still the difficult charge. I find that presidents are looking for catchy words and creative solutions and believe they need to accomplish this alone. This is the perfect place to get some help! Whether you choose some very creative faculty or staff members, or you survey the possibilities for external help, it is essential not to feel alone in this endeavor.

There is an old question that is often used to stimulate thinking in this area: "What would you like the headlines to be 10 years from now when people write about your college or university?" The question is still relevant, and it appears to bring everyone's thinking to a more focused place. This exercise requires careful attention and creativity to take those thoughts to the next level. The thoughtfulness in this process usually allows a concise and compelling result to rise to the surface.

SUMMARY

The inclusion of a focus on vision in our thriving framework is largely because of the fact that thriving colleges have been able to get this right. They have amended and refined their mission statements to embrace tradition and describe the foundation that is relevant. They have clearly and concisely crafted a vision statement that is a compelling inspiration to all constituencies. Their core values are alive and well on campus. When you talk to members of the campus community, there is no question about what they do, where they are going, and why they do what they do. The unity and connection are apparent, and improve the institutional self-esteem. Thriving colleges are happy places to work, and the mission, vision, and core values live at the center of all they do.

DISCUSSION QUESTIONS:

VISION

- Does your institution have a clear mission statement?
- Has the mission statement been updated in the last five years?
- Is there a clear vision statement?
- Do you believe the campus community is aware of the vision statement?
- If you have a vision statement, is it closely connected to your strategic initiatives?
- When strategic decisions are made at the president's cabinet level, are they directly related to the shared vision for the future?
- Was the board of trustees involved in the development of the vision statement?
- Do the marketing materials of the institution clearly articulate the vision?
- Was there a process implemented inside of the campus community to gain "buy in" for the vision?

Chapter 4

Institutional Self-Esteem

When questioned about the morale on campus, one president said to me, "Don't ever mention morale to me again! On every campus in the world, the morale is either bad or the worst it has ever been!" I had not been consulting for very long at that time, and I believed him. As time has gone by, though, I've changed my mind. There are clearly some campuses that glow with pride. To keep schools from getting caught in negativity, I talk to them about the concept of institutional self-esteem – it's that feeling that shows up on college campuses as excitement and motivation. As our team at Credo was doing the research to test the nine elements present in thriving colleges, this one stood out as a true driver of success. Thriving colleges and universities are paying attention to some key building blocks of pride that make institutional self-esteem possible, and even inevitable.

SEVEN BUILDERS OF INSTITUTIONAL SELF-ESTEEM

Know Your Students – They are YOURS!

This seems so simple, but it is always paramount to know who your students are. Understanding their preparation and where they come from is important for marketing purposes, but it is even more important in planning for the learning environment necessary for them to thrive. There is considerable research that supports a model for positive engagement of students, rather than analyzing their areas of deficit (Schreiner, Noel, Anderson, & Cantwell, 2011). Developing the right instructional model for the students you have is key to their success.

Thriving colleges embrace the students that they recruit. Whether students are from Chicago, Birmingham, or Shanghai, the entire campus community believes in the students they recruit and the potential they have (Barlett & Fischer, 2011). The endless pursuit of better students is not what makes a thriving college! Institutions with low self-esteem continue to press that conversation forward instead of driving energy into providing for the students they have.

Where are Your Shining Stars?

Thriving colleges have been able to identify their stars and tell their stories well. This goes beyond the accomplishment of individuals to the accomplishments of groups, whether they are athletic teams or debate teams. Generally, I have not seen small private colleges and universities leveraging their shining stars well.

The stories of these people, teams, and initiatives are encouraging, and stimulate pride throughout the campus. There is nothing that makes us happier than the success of those who belong to us! Frequently I will ask a group of leaders at an institution to name

10 to 15 of these stories for me spontaneously. Usually the group can identify four or five clear instances of success, but after that it becomes murky. The thriving institutions are constantly looking for these stories and lifting them up to all constituencies. The stories and the people in the stories are products of our brand promise. We cannot afford to neglect them. They are a critical component of the value proposition.

> The stories and the people in the stories are products of our brand promise. We cannot afford to neglect them. They are part of the value proposition.

We Need Proof!

Outcome stories are different than the stories of our stars. We are being driven to accumulate outcomes by everyone, from the government to the parents of students. The federal government is crafting more and more legislation that requires greater transparency and clarity around return on investment (Supiano, 2012). It is no longer possible for us to charge and collect the tuition fees we publish if we are not going to pay careful attention to the value proposition we offer. Our conversations about warm, friendly campuses and caring faculty have run their course. Who would have thought 30 years ago that we would read an article in *The Chronicle of Higher Education* entitled "Is ROI the Right Way to Judge a College Education?" (Carlson, 2013)?

We must be able to show results, and most of those results have to have a number in them. It is important for parents to know that 87% of all freshmen at your institution have been involved in internships. It is important for them to know that 92% of all biology majors are accepted into medical and veterinary schools, and from which schools they received acceptances. It's also important for us to think about our adult students. Their graduation rates, job prospects, and increases in their incomes are important numbers necessary to persuade them to embrace more education. Last, but certainly not least, donors to our institutions are looking for concrete ways to see that they are a part of something significant and successful. Today's donors are increasingly referred to as venture philanthropists, looking for measurable deliverables in return for their donations (LeFrance & Lathan, 2008). It is simply impossible for us to do the work we do any longer without talking about the results.

Coming and Staying

There is nothing that says pride more than the largest freshman class ever, and the largest percentage of them staying for the next year. This will never change. We will always be gauging our success based on our ability to attract students. For many years, hitting freshman enrollment goals was the biggest indicator of institutional self-esteem, but now it is crystal clear: if those students do not *stay*, we have been neglectful. We must continue to emphasize increases in retention and graduation numbers with the same fervor with which we count the members of the freshman class. We are bound to do this both by our dedication to the revenue streams that help us accomplish mission, and by our dedication to the students who come to us with the uninhibited hope that they can succeed.

This new push is demonstrated by the fact that more and more colleges and universities are expanding their retention efforts (Supiano, 2009). Students returning to us equals a job well done. It lifts everyone's spirits. We will talk later about the revenue stream increases through small percentage-point differences in retention.

Any increases in revenue from new and returning students boosts self-esteem exponentially.

Spend the Money in the Right Places!

Over the years there have been many jokes about the fact that a crane on campus means a thriving college or university. This isn't too far off track! Thriving colleges are visibly reinvesting in people, places, and programs. They have made it clear to the faculty and staff that they are appreciated and rewarded based on their accomplishments. They have taken fresh looks at their academic and co-curricular programs, are making investments in them, and are building or remodeling spaces that encourage engagement. They are continuing to improve, and in the right places!

It's difficult to understand budgeting in higher education, and probably not a valuable undertaking for most members of the campus community. But when things are going well, or when they're not, it's easy to discern priorities by watching where the money goes. Faculty and staff are keenly aware of these allocations. Best practice dictates investing surplus funds, and even budgeted funds, with a focus on the strategic initiatives that have been clearly identified and affirmed by the board of trustees and the campus community. Moving off-plan for special agendas opens the door for institutional self-esteem to take a dive. When it is clear that money is being spent in the places that make the most difference according to careful, collaborative strategic planning, then self-esteem *always* takes a step up (Bryson, 2011).

Celebrate and Appreciate!

Thriving colleges celebrate, and they celebrate frequently! They are amazingly good at leveraging every small victory. They have learned that internal marketing is as important as external marketing. Kotter emphasizes that even small wins are central in gaining precious momentum (2012). These schools grab onto outcomes and data points and make them clear and visible, both verbally and in print, and they continually lift up the successes of campus community members.

Although the little things are very important, the thriving colleges are also celebrating in big ways. They have paid careful attention to traditions, convocations, special speakers, and sparkling performing arts experiences. They thrive on providing times for the community to gather. Some have weekly traditions, encouraging faculty, staff, and students to mingle at designated times. Others have been very deliberate about providing more and better spaces so groups and organizations can gather and celebrate more frequently. While some institutions recognize employees through salary increases, Garvey (2005) highlights that non-financial forms of appreciation can be just as impactful, if not more so. From the perfect branded items to upgraded graduation regalia, items of pride are carefully and strategically planned. Appreciation is essential, and the culture is built around it. There are more special awards opportunities for more people in the thriving colleges, and the senior leadership takes time to know and encourage each person.

More People, More Involved!

The word *engagement* is used constantly on our campuses as it relates to a student's educational journey. When students engage at higher levels, learning and morale increases. We should also look closely at the engagement of our faculty and staff, and their relationship to our students. Self-esteem increases when institutions have engaged additional constituencies at the highest level. This means that parents are clearly informed and excited about what they see and hear through a strategic communications plan. It means that donors are being cared for at the best levels of stewardship, and their numbers are increasing.

It also means that city leaders and residents are proud of *their* institution, and show it by attending events, supporting partnerships, and offering internships at increasing levels. When conversations in the community are instead laced with hard questions and frequent criticism, institutional self-esteem is under attack. The relationship of a college or university to its home community is usually a direct result of presidential engagement. If a president has made this a priority, then great encouragement comes from friends and neighbors speaking positively about the institution to faculty and staff.

When institutional self-esteem is low, planning is often immobilized. Action is stagnant. Innovation is crushed. College administrators are distracted by hours of time spent listening to complaints and discouragement. An even worse side effect is our natural inclination to move into silos. The default position for conscientious educators who believe their institution to be surviving instead of thriving will be to retreat to a familiar corner where they are sure they can make a difference. I often hear our leaders talk about silos, and criticize their existence as if faculty and staff purposely stay separated. They complain that programs and services must be more integrated. I'm well aware, though, that many good faculty and staff members are driven to their corners by poor planning and a lack of institutional self-esteem.

SUMMARY

It is as important to pay attention to internal communication as external communication! And it seems to be more difficult because we do not have clear positions dedicated to monitoring the building of community on our campuses. These staff positions are seen as non-essential, and are the last to be funded. I am becoming more and more sure that we are going to have to pay careful attention to this if we are going to make the changes in the academy that we need to make at this time in history. Strong institutional self-esteem will carry us a long way toward being able to innovate and mobilize for success!

DISCUSSION QUESTIONS:

INSTITUTIONAL SELF-ESTEEM

- Do the employees at your institution truly believe that they have the capability to enact positive change?
- Do you frequently see examples of institutional pride among the campus community?
- Is there a tradition of meeting or exceeding your enrollment goals?
- Is there a tradition of meeting or exceeding your freshman-to-sophomore retention goals?
- Is there a tradition of meeting or exceeding your graduation rate goals?
- Has it been necessary to cut salary and/or benefits for faculty or staff over the last three years?
- Are stories of success about students, faculty, and staff being lifted up on a consistent basis?

- Have you had any recent national or regional visibility for distinctive programs, successes, wins, and celebrations?
- Are you consistently communicating points of institutional pride internally?
- Are you consistently communicating points of institutional pride externally?
- Is the campus kept well-manicured and landscaped?
- Is there obvious deferred maintenance on campus?
- Are you able to recruit and retain high-quality faculty and staff?
- Are there readily available examples of alumni who have had notable accomplishments?
- Is there a general feeling of well-being and good morale among campus consistencies?
- Does the institution seem to have a "silo" culture?
- Do people feel overworked, and not like they are accomplishing significant initiatives?

Chapter 5

Institutional Story

I will never forget walking behind a tour guide at an institution with a beautiful swimming pool. She was talking about her college, and was obviously very proud. I was taken with her enthusiasm, and believed with all my heart that the family she was touring would probably make a decision that day because of her influence. Another 100 feet later, she began to tell a story about the nationally ranked swim team at the institution. It was a Cinderella story – the team was new, had come from behind, and was now nationally ranked. It took my breath away, but not because she was continuing her spectacular relationship with the family. The reason for my lack of oxygen was that there was not, in fact, a swim team at this college! She was not unlike the rest of us. We are all a little confused about the story to tell to our constituencies.

This is one of many examples that illustrate the difficulty we have getting our institutional story straight. Campus tour guides aside, if you asked 10 dedicated faculty and staff members to script a one-minute story about your institution, you would likely receive 10 versions, and some of the facts would not be accurate. Part of the complexity here is that we are all looking for a silver bullet. We want to say just the right words at just the right time to inspire internal constituencies about the institution, and to attract prospective students and donors to it.

The ability of your leaders, faculty, staff, and students to share a consistent institutional story is necessary in today's higher education marketplace. With increased competition for resources, colleges and universities are feeling pressure to make lots of promises to students. But if they cannot deliver on those promises, they will feel the backlash in dropping retention.

We must remember that marketing is still in its infancy on many campuses. While higher education in America was established over 300 years ago, it was not until 1972 that Krachenberg wrote "Bringing the Concept of Marketing to Higher Education." In 2003, Naddaff was quoted as saying, "branding...is not a dirty word any more" (Pulley, 2003, para. 9). Progress is being made, but the infrastructure for marketing our institutions it is still being built.

As this growth area for schools demands more focused attention, confusion about marketing terms and elements is real, and could lead to expensive errors. To guide your process, you'll find basic definitions throughout this chapter that contextualize the role and significance of the elements of marketing as it relates to colleges and universities.

Amidst the need for growth and clarity around marketing in higher education, the urgency of telling your institutional story well has never been more important. For tuition-driven institutions, the effectiveness of marketing is ultimately judged by enrollment and retention, and to a *much* lesser extent, fundraising. You can have solid programs, strong faculty, a beautiful campus, and a unique focus, but if you are not consistently communicating

> It is imperative for campus marketing departments to keep time and investment centered on attracting and retaining students.

your story internally and externally to various constituencies, key indicators for success will *not* move. Many things vie for time in a campus marketing office that will not move the needle on a strategic scorecard. It is imperative for campus marketing departments to keep time and investment centered on attracting and retaining students.

ORGANIZING FOR SUCCESS

Thriving colleges recognize the importance of naming marketing as a key department on campus, allocating resources appropriately, and including its leader in the presidential cabinet. They have embraced an agency model for the delivery of their marketing services, treating departments and campus offices as clients. They are organized to prioritize marketing initiatives around recruiting students, retaining them, and securing financial resources. Their marketing dollars have been centralized, removing the temptation of other offices to create and disseminate messages or visuals that are inconsistent with the institutional brand.

The marketing department at a college can be one of the most overwhelmed. When it isn't organized correctly, it becomes the dumping ground for every individual faculty or staff member who would like a brochure. The ability to embrace user-friendly technology to do much of the internal work and promotion will be key to releasing marketing experts for core initiatives.

I have seen many marketing organization charts over the years. Private colleges have a huge range of diversity in this area. Many still function with one person who handles all marketing communications activities and publications, while others have designated positions for internal clients and have outsourced their most prestigious marketing pieces. Some are so well-staffed that they do all marketing projects in-house, though most colleges and universities outsource their branding and positioning work. The culture of the institution should determine how best to organize in this regard, as long as clear strategy and an agency approach are still at the heart of the operation.

Leadership is crucial in this area. The chief marketing officer on campus should be skilled at listening and giving clear expectations to internal clients. He or she should also have expert knowledge about the value of market research, and be passionate about segmenting the market in focused ways. It is essential for marketing leaders to act as an advocate for quality, investment and focus throughout the institution's marketing efforts. A school's marketing leader has the responsibility to go to bed at night and wake up in the morning with the image and reputation of his or her institution at the forefront.

MARKET RESEARCH: DO YOUR HOMEWORK!

Thriving colleges know exactly what kind of students they want to recruit, and the messages they want to communicate to them. They know where their best prospects are, and what they like. They know what stops some of them from enrolling, and they know where they go if they don't enroll. They have the ability to understand where there is whitespace in the market, and whether they can deliver a program well.

There is no secret to gaining this knowledge! Investing in market research is essential, and cannot be overlooked. Thriving colleges conduct the research needed to obtain a better handle on options that can bring a return on investment. Their marketing departments are then able to deliver recommendations for investments that result in successful enrollment. While market research has become an essential exercise in higher education, I'm afraid we are still not incredibly savvy in this area. You will succeed more often by demanding research before designating marketing dollars.

Market Research: The tools and processes used to examine current market realities and constituency perceptions. Among many things, market research provides a solid data platform from which to launch the branding process.

In one market research project at a small private college, students ranked one of our clients as being VERY good at character development, but when asked how important character development was to them in their choice of college, it ranked at the very lowest level of importance. The lesson is: if you're great at it, but your stakeholders don't think it's important, then it's not a strong marketing point! If no one cares, then it shouldn't be part of your story. Researchers Anderson, Narus, & van Rossum emphasize that internal stakeholders often see more value in what their organizations have to offer than consumers do (2006). They write that organizational leaders "may claim advantages for features that actually provide no benefit to target customers" (p. 92).

One can see how an institution's story can get off track. Market research is an especially important tool in determining current reality and setting benchmark data against which future progress can be measured. It also uncovers what key constituencies know about you, what misperceptions they may have about you, what they find unique about you, and how they define your competitive set. The results may not be what you expect! Once you have that brand knowledge, you can begin the work of building positive associations, (re)defining who you are, and delivering unique messages and desired experiences.

BRAND: DEFINE YOUR STORY!

What *is* your institutional story? Is it your values? Your mission? Your sports team? The truth is, it's none of these. Your institutional story is essentially your brand.

Presidents have called Credo and said, "We don't have a brand." That's never true – brand is not your logo, or your viewbook, or your school mascot, though all of these things are *representations* of your brand. While a great deal of time and energy are spent on these brand representations, and they are key in *sharing* your story, they do not position your institution in the marketplace in the same way that research-based brand knowledge does. Your *brand* is the sum of perceptions you and others have about your institution, and those perceptions are reality (Keller, 2012).

> **Brand:** The sum total of all external and internal associations made about your institution. The current state of your brand can be determined by targeted market research.

> **Branding:** The process of influencing the associations with your brand.

One of the outcomes of serious market research should be the development of positioning statements, a brief series of sentences that provide the baseline context for all of your external marketing messaging, and light the path for continuing to shape your brand. Positioning statements are for internal use, not for splashing on billboards – their language should be *slightly* aspirational, a good balance between the current reality and the desired experience.

Positioning Statement: This is your internal roadmap for external messaging. Positioning statement(s) are based on current perceptions compared to current realities and aspirations.

Your institutional story or brand should transcend transitions in leadership to maintain consistency. It should not change every time a new president is appointed. This is challenging, because the average presidential tenure at private colleges and universities is about seven years (Song & Hartley, 2012). In general industry, the average tenure of chief marketing officers is only 28 months, the least of any c-level executives (Linton, 2009). Neither of these trends provides a strong foundation for a brand strategy that may need to last more than a decade, so your brand must itself be strong, and rooted in your institutional identity.

VALUE PROPOSITION

Some private colleges get caught in the trap of trying to prove affordability above all else. Focusing on your value proposition – outcomes versus cost – places the strengths of your institutional brand at the forefront, and frames the conversation around value. Strategies of value are preferred over low-cost pricing (Raynor & Ahmed, 2013).

Value Proposition: This is the perception of cost as compared to outcomes. Schools with a strong value proposition are not necessarily inexpensive, but their cost is perceived as an excellent value for the outcomes provided by the experience.

The outcome stories we pointed to as significant in the journey to strong institutional self-esteem are, without a doubt, the clearest, strongest pieces of your institutional story, and are the focal point of your value proposition. Small private colleges and universities can never compete with state schools on cost, but those schools will have a difficult time matching private colleges and universities on transformational experiences and outcomes (Vedder, 2004). Effectively sharing student outcomes connects the successes of your alumni to the hopes of your prospective students, reinforcing your value proposition.

$$value = what\ I\ get\ /\ what\ I\ pay$$

OUTCOMES, OUTCOMES, OUTCOMES!

It is impossible to think about marketing messages and branding without the help of specific outcomes. Outcome stories and outcome metrics have become crucial to our marketing efforts. I feel like I need to write that 10 times in a row. It seems like it is one of the most difficult things to do because we still don't see them enough!! They are critical drivers for telling the institutional story. Following are some important things to remember about outcomes:

- Outcome stories need to be compelling, but also show an accurate representation of your institutional experience, and should be consistent with mission-vision-values.

- The majority of private colleges do not have the internal infrastructure or systems in place to collect outcomes or undertake comprehensive market research. Get help!
- Partnerships between marketing professionals and faculty members are key to obtaining personal outcome and success stories. Marketing staff members have to take the lead, but an institutional priority must be proclaimed about outcome so there are no obstacles to obtaining them.
- Always tell outcomes across all channels. Reuse them, recycle them, repackage them. They are difficult to obtain and refine, so reuse them unabashedly!
- Qualitative outcomes (human stories) and quantitative outcomes (metrics) are both important. Example: 95% of nursing students got licensure, and here's a story about a nursing student who changed someone's life.
- Market research continues to show that one of the most important outcomes for higher education is the ability to secure a good job following graduation (Jaschik, 2013, Tankersley, 2013), so finding and sharing career stories is critical.
- Outcomes provide accountability.

SEGMENTATION

Once you know your brand and have collected sparkling outcomes stories to share with your constituents, you must begin to break down those constituent groups into relevant categories and tie appropriate messaging to the marketing information they will receive. Colleges and universities continue to send bulk marketing pieces to thousands of students without segmenting them, and without proven knowledge about what they would like to hear and see. "Branding in the Digital Age: You're Spending Your Money in all the Wrong Places" (Edelman, 2010) highlights the importance of investing marketing dollars that align with the habits and preferences of your target audiences. A lack of market segmentation can mean that millions of dollars are misdirected toward unfruitful marketing endeavors.

> **Segmentation:** The ability to speak more directly to individually identified audiences WHILE STILL BEING CONSISTENT and true to the overall brand.

Sometimes one of our team members will stop by my office to show me something they have developed for a college or university, and they are proud of it. My first thought is that if I like it, we are in big trouble! I am smart enough to know that all marketing materials designed to be delivered to traditional students, adult students, alumni, and other key groups better be tested directly with them to see what resonates. It just doesn't matter what resonates with me. It is my hope that presidents will assume that position. There have been way too many marketing packages resting on the approval of college presidents.

Brand researchers of all varieties agree that first and foremost, marketing and branding must be viewed from the viewpoint of the customer. Keller notes that a strong brand "excels at delivering the benefits customers truly desire" (2000, p. 148). Brand is in the eye of the beholder, and that beholder is the enrolling student.

SUMMARY

You will be well served to develop a set of marketing messages that distinguish you in the marketplace and help tell your institutional story, and then integrate them into everything you do! The organization of your marketing team will be instrumental in that endeavor. You must use market research to determine the correct set of messages for the correct set of people. We hear a lot these days about elevator speeches, but the truth is that the elevator speech depends upon who you are in the elevator with!

In the end, the most important story of all is about the success of your students. We will never be able to continue asking families to sacrifice for this investment unless the value proposition is strong, and our messages are clear and targeted enough to carry it to the right people at the right time.

DISCUSSION QUESTIONS:
INSTITUTIONAL STORY

- Has your campus been through a branding process?
- Do you know the "brand" of your institution?
- Are your marketing and communication efforts centralized?
- Do you have strong, visible marketing leadership?
- Is there a member of the leadership team with strong marketing responsibilities?
- Is your brand promise mission-driven?
- Is your board aware of your brand promise?
- Is your cabinet aware of your brand promise?
- Is your brand promise clear to external constituencies?

- Is your brand positioning statement clear internally to the campus community?
- Is your brand strong enough to withstand significant leadership changes?
- Do you feel that the admissions staff would tell the same story about your institution as your faculty would?
- Do you use timely research data to drive your marketing strategy?
- Do you have a set of core marketing messages that distinguish you from your competitors?
- Do you know how key constituencies perceive you?
- Do you regularly collect outcomes from graduates?
- Are the stories of success at your institution accumulated and shared as a part of your brand?
- Do you have an internal positioning strategy (marketing roadmap)?
- Are the messages shared across target groups consistent?
- Do you have the ability to segment marketing messages based on targeted audiences?
- Do your marketing materials clearly articulate your institutional brand?

Chapter 6

Habit of Reflection & Intentionality

Sometimes it feels like I am a part of that old telephone game we used to play when we were kids. We used to stand in a line, maybe four or five of us, and one of us would tell a story and whisper it to the next person. Do you remember it? By the time the story got to the end of the line, it was completely different.

I have felt that way many times while sitting in a planning session with a president. I will ask a question about a key indicator of college success. It might be a retention rate, a number of thousand-dollar donors, the current number of deposited students, or even the number students graduating. The president picks up the phone and calls someone and gets a number. Moments later the phone rings, that person has asked another person, and they have a different number. Then the president asks a strategic question about the number and hangs up. Fifteen minutes later, there is a new caller with a new number!

There is so much valuable data right in front of us. Despite many demands on our time, creating space for reflection on what our data is telling us is crucial. Once we have interpreted it, we must be intentional about using it effectively. The data will always be valuable in determining what we ought to do new and what we ought to do differently. An even more strategic move toward thriving would be to use all this data to encourage ourselves and embrace what we do well!

NUMBERS, NUMBERS EVERYWHERE

How does your data look? Everywhere you turn, there is talk about data, and campuses need to make sure they are in on the conversation. People call it data-based, data-driven, or data-informed decision-making (Davenport, 2013). Sometimes other terms include analytics, decision support, and business intelligence. In a 2012 research study, 84% of higher education leaders reported that analytics are more important than two years ago. Similarly, 86% reported that in two years, analytics will be more important than they are today (Bichsel, 2012).

I used to staunchly defend the notion that in education we can't measure everything, but we don't live in that world anymore. From the parents of the students we recruit to the adults who study online with us, everyone is looking for outcomes. Accreditation and governmental agencies will continue to press institutions for greater clarity regarding strategic data (Hebel, 2008). We simply must be able to measure what we do. In a 2009 address, Secretary of Education Arne Duncan said:

The common denominator for all of these policy decisions was that they were informed by data. I am a deep believer in the power of data to drive our decisions. Data gives us the roadmap to reform. It tells us where we are, where we need to go.

My co-author Rick often talks about three kinds of data:

1. The first kind of data is **data we already have.** It is right at our fingertips and we know exactly where to go when we want to quote it or use it.
2. The second kind of data is **data that is around**, but we don't quite have our hands on it. It doesn't take much for us to go and find it, but we don't keep it handy and we're often not sure where it is when we need it.
3. The third kind of data is **data we don't have at all**. We will have to find a way to get it, and that takes time.

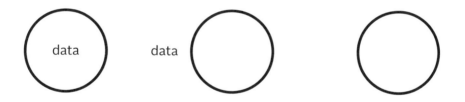

I love Rick's analysis of this. It has helped us talk to colleges about the data dilemma. But whether the data is here, around somewhere, or not here at all, the biggest controversy for me as I watch colleges and universities attempt to make good use of it is related to *quality*.

We have survived for years on lagging indicators in the academy. A semester or a year goes by and we look back to see how we have done. For many institutions, the most common analysis is an annual report that is almost completely backwards-looking. We are often surprised when enrollment numbers don't come in exactly as we predicted, and very surprised when retention is down. It is time for us to embrace leading indicators as the important strategic ingredients, the drivers of our strategy (Niven, 2008). Leading indicators are the metrics that help us to improve, and give us the ability to make corrections midstream.

Finding good metrics used to be a mystery to me, but it has gotten clearer and clearer. For example, we have available to us four clear ways to measure what we do:

1. **Raw numbers,** such as total enrollment.
2. **Ratios**, such as our student/faculty ratio.
3. **Rubrics** that can give meaning to qualitative data, such as feedback on courses, housing, or writing quality.
4. **Percentages** that show relationships, such as graduation and retention rates, percentage of minority faculty, or year-to-date percentage of alumni giving.

The need for better data process and strategic application does not mean that every college or university leader needs to become an expert quantitative analyst. Instead, leaders need to champion a growing data-informed culture (Niven, 2008), and become skilled consumers of data analytics (Davenport, 2013). This can include learning or refreshing your knowledge of the basics of data types and statistics, developing a deeper understanding of hypothesis framing and testing, and soliciting knowledge from those on your staff with data expertise. If you feel uncomfortable talking with your team, have a consultant coach you through these concepts and processes.

Remember that collecting data and keeping track of metrics is only useful if we have chosen the right ones connected with campus strategy, and have defined them clearly and correctly so there is never an argument about their validity. Arguments about the credibility of data can be a huge distraction.

DASHBOARDS AND SCORECARDS

It would be safe to say that the new buzzword around board meetings these days is *dashboard*. When we started to talk about dashboards several years ago, I think everybody got excited about the fact that we would have our hands on the wheel of data analysis, but having our hands on the wheel means that the dashboards will need to be relevant, appropriate, and current – all the more reason to be careful about which data we report and how we report it. Increasingly, organizations are moving toward dashboards and scorecards with accompanying visual reporting (Bishsel, 2012). With such movement, there is a distinct need the need for connecting data with strategy (Lunger, 2006). Dashboards tend to be used more for short-term data, while scorecards provide a more long-term strategic focus.

I've asked several presidents to show me their dashboards. I've seen dashboards that were all done in PowerPoint or Excel. One institution had a dashboard with 54 indicators, and each indicator had seven to nine numbers. That's over 400 data points in one dashboard! That's impossible for people to digest, and would certainly not reassure me as to the strategic direction of my institution if I were a board of trustees member.

A better approach is a balanced scorecard, which is limited to 10 – 20 strategic objectives with accompanying measures. This amount of data in visual form is manageable. The more information we are able to give our board members in a simple and concise way, the more trust we will see. As I mentioned in the chapter on courageous leadership, trust and credibility in higher education leadership will be the key to board members embracing their roles effectively and appropriately. To meet that need, a balanced scorecard can be a powerful tool.

Balanced scorecards are currently used by more than half of Fortune 500 companies and continue to be viewed as a key strategic tool (Rigby & Bilobeau, 2011). Research continues to show that both for-profit and nonprofit organizations using a balanced scorecard outperform those that do not (Christesen, 2008; Greatbanks & Tapp, 2007). At Credo, both internally and externally, we use the balanced scorecard method as a guide for how we assess, plan, and deliver. We'll discuss this more in the *Culture of Planning and Innovation* chapter. The simple reassurance that the clarity of purpose and correct measurement will be there on all recommendations is now essential to us. I absolutely love showing a president, staff, faculty, and board a meter that shows them what they have accomplished and how far they need to go.

BETTER THAN LAST YEAR

There has been much conversation over the past years about benchmarking and higher education. We have become ravenous for information that will tell us what other colleges are doing. It has been fascinating to watch this hunger accelerate to new levels. The discouragement around the lack of benchmarking data has distracted us from the more relevant conversation about continuous improvement.

Everybody needs to do better, regardless of the status quo. I am reminded of recent conversations at two colleges about the freshman-to-sophomore fall-to-fall retention rate. The rates at both of those universities were between 65 and 70%. Long discussions ensued, with a focus on what other colleges' and universities' rates might be. As I reach the age of retirement, I have less and less tolerance for conversations that do not lead to action. It seems very simple to me that those conversations need to be about moving up three or four percentage points and how to do that, rather than ongoing speculation about other schools.

> Our discussions must run parallel to our actions, and our actions must be swift and relevant to the goals of continuous improvement.

That said, thoughtful comparisons can be helpful for deepening thought around these data issues (Guan, Nunez, & Welsh, 2002). First, we begin to see greater clarity in the data from our own institutions. Second, it brings clarity on how we define success. What are our retention numbers, average course size, endowment values? Data clarity and benchmarking allow for more productive comparisons to past performance, peer institutions, and aspirant institutions.

It can be difficult in this environment to develop a good list of peer and aspirant institutions. Schools have often drawn outside of the lines just a bit and worked very hard at finding distinctiveness. That is a worthy endeavor, but it makes comparing ourselves with like institutions more challenging. The greater and more effective comparison is an internal one – identifying where we were last year and celebrating where we are this year. Again, urgency prevails. Our discussions must run parallel to our actions, and our actions must be swift and relevant to the goals of continuous improvement.

THE "A" WORD

I can't remember the first time I heard the word *assessment*, but I know that I haven't been on a college campus in fifteen years when it hasn't been in the conversation. Our accrediting agencies were ahead of us when they jumped into this world, and they have demanded that we find a way to prove that we do what we say we do. Assessment continues to require increasingly large amounts of time, personnel, and money. Additionally, accreditation is gaining more and more attention from the federal government (Eaton, 2010). Related to this federal oversight is the growing role of the student as consumer (Eaton, 2012). While the assessment focus of accreditation agencies in the past two decades has grown rapidly, the currents in this direction may be even stronger in the decade to come (Kelderman, 2013).

Our next challenge will be to use the material and information we have collected in the great assessment movement to assist us in getting better at everything we do, i.e., intentional implementation of strategies based on relevant data. Recently, a family visited me with a high school senior son who was interested in history. When asked how they might find the right college for him with a superior program in history, I advised them to talk to the chairs of several history departments about graduate outcomes. After five visits, the family informed me that information was not available about these graduates. This is unacceptable in today's higher education climate! Institutions must improve their ability to access and share outcomes as a result of quality assessment. We must reflect on what we have done, and use it to attract, teach, and retain the students we love so dearly.

DO YOUR RESEARCH

Arbitrary or anecdotal opinions should not provide the foundation for determining strategy. As we discussed in the *Institutional Story* chapter, market research might be the most important kind of data and reflection tool that we have embraced over these last few decades in higher education. Reflecting on market research has become important in the development of new programs, in the projection of enrollment numbers, and in developing strategy. Intentionally surveying the groups of people that we want to serve and analyzing the results is essential to the future.

WE DID SOMETHING RIGHT!

At a time when we are becoming more and more discouraged about making a difference, the celebration of data points are almost absent. When I read the questions on the Student Satisfaction Inventory (SSI) and the National Survey of Student Engagement (NSSE), and then look at the positive responses possible, I'm convinced that we have missed opportunities to share and celebrate.

One of the best practices that I've come to love is the intentionality of college leadership teams who take a day each semester to celebrate significant data points. These days are fascinating to watch. Each member of the president's cabinet studies the data that has come to his/her attention and brings it to the day. It doesn't come to the table without discernment. It is lifted up for its relevance, strategic, and celebratory value.

SUMMARY

Data points are overwhelming! When we do information requests at colleges, we are shocked at the amount of data they are accumulating and gathering. I will leave you with four important points to consider as you immerse yourself in the new era of obsession about data collections:

1. **Decide** what you want to collect.
2. **Collect** it and analyze it so it is useful to you in your work.
3. **Act** on it with corrective measures so you can continually improve.
4. **Celebrate** it when it shows you have done something wonderful!

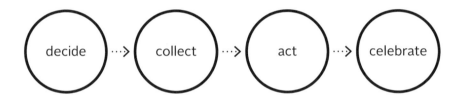

DISCUSSION QUESTIONS:
HABIT OF REFLECTION & INTENTIONALITY

- Is there an identified full-time position for institutional research?
- Do you share data with appropriate constituencies for celebratory purposes?
- Are there specified times set aside for the president's cabinet for reflecting on assessment metrics and strategizing from the results?
- Do you use data to make strategic institutional decisions?

- Is there a centralized process at your institution by which data is collected, reviewed and shared?
- Do you share data with appropriate constituencies for celebratory purposes?
- Do you have a robust assessment plan for academic departments?
- Do you have a robust assessment plan for administrative departments?
- Are there data at your institution that are collected and not used for strategic purposes?
- Are the decisions for adding and deleting academic programs based upon research and data?
- Do you survey students to understand their satisfaction level?
- Do you use predictive modeling to segment markets in your enrollment division?
- Do you use market research before beginning new programs?
- Do you use market research before opening satellite locations?

Chapter 7

Culture of Planning & Innovation

"That is not an objective, it's a goal! No, it's an initiative... No, it's an imperative... No, it's a project... No, it's a task!"

"Strategic planning is just plain wearisome. Our campus is tired of it."

"If this plan is not going to say something about my department expanding, then I don't want to be a part of the planning."

"I had thousands of the plan printed in full-color. Now can you come and help me get buy-in from the college community? I did the plan myself last summer."

"We have the possibility of a $20,000,000 gift for international education, but it isn't in our strategic plan."

"We cannot even start this process until we know who we are. We have a mission and vision statement, but we still don't know who we are."

"There is no point in planning. We have no money."

"You simply can't measure that. I know it's the right thing to do, but there is no way to measure it."

"I think the goose poop on the sidewalks is one of the biggest internal threats we have right now."

"There is no point in looking ahead at opportunities for the future. Our best bet is to look at everything that is wrong here."

In all my years of consulting, I've learned that anything can happen in strategic planning! As you can see in the actual client quotes above, institutions come to this process with questions about readiness and identity, weariness over finances and current challenges, and yes, concerns about goose poop.

There is no way to even count the methods that have been used in private higher education over the past decades. Something different happens in every college or university, but there are common threads of thought and action. Since I began facilitating strategic planning processes, the same issues have come up over and over. I imagine you have encountered some of these on your own campuses!

DON'T MAJOR ON THE MINOR!

I announced about five years ago that I was never going to argue about words during a strategic planning session again. There is often a great deal of passion and energy focused on whether something is called a *goal* or an *objective*. Those are the two big words. An understanding of the nuances of planning words is irrelevant. Just choose the ones that you would like to use in your setting and stick to them.

Really, the core concepts and the planning itself are the important things. It is important to review mission. It is important to cast new vision. It is important for many schools to define the values embraced by the campus community. After that, it's all about stating where you are going, what is most important, how you are going to get there, and how you are going to measure progress. You can call those things anything that feels right to you. We offer some suggestions later in this chapter, but choose whatever is right for your culture and let the words go!

PLANNING IS MESSY, AND NECESSARY!

Generating excitement and ideas, and refining them until you are focused on the four or five things that could make the most difference to an institution is not an easy process. There will never be enough conversation, and someone will always believe that something is missing. The plan will never be written or mapped to everyone's expectation. There will be ambiguity as ideas and dreams are brought to the table. When you put that together with the multiple personalities and working styles of faculty and staff, it is inevitable that someone will say he or she is totally confused! I dread the moment in time when that happens. I always know it's coming, and it takes the wind out of the room. While strategic planning has its detractors (Shrader, Taylor, & Dalton, 1984), most recent research documents its many benefits (Bryson, 2011). These benefits include promotion of strategic thinking, improved decision-making, enhanced organizational effectiveness, and direct benefits to people involved (Bryson, 2010), and this holds true for planning in higher education (Alfred, 2006). There is also a general trend toward campus stakeholders feeling an increased need for strategic planning (Welsh, Nunez, & Petrosko, 2005).

Planning leaders must pay special attention to connecting the dots after each planning session. There is nothing worse than campus-wide rumors about how the planning is going nowhere. When done well, strategic planning is clearly worth the time, effort, and costs.

Planning has a Reputation!

It is amazing how a planning process can suffer from the reputation of the process preceding it. There is double jeopardy if the process was bad *and* the plan was never executed. The strategic process will be more difficult and meet with more obstacles if some of the history is not aired and put to rest! Knowing the reputation of planning on your campus is important, but it should not impede forward motion. One of my favorite things to do when I'm asked to assist in strategic planning is to gather together the planning history and all of the documents important to it. I love to look at where everyone has been. I love even more to present a clear picture of continually improving processes that are more efficient, collaborative, and transparent.

Who's on First?

The discussion about who should lead strategic planning efforts is an interesting one. It doesn't neatly fall into anyone's territory. There are, however, many prejudices about this. Some feel very strongly that the president of the college must lead the process. Others believe it is the role of the chief academic officer. I believe planning leadership should fall to the best facilitators who have a strong skillset in leading change and are respected on campus. Many times planning processes don't start because people are not quite sure who should lead them. Organizations have to actively bring together people who can lead change effectively (Kotter, 2012). These people are not always the president or vice presidents. Instead, these are teams of people who can be catalytic and collaborative in leading change.

WHAT WILL IT LOOK LIKE?

When I walk into the first planning meeting at a college, there are 100 things on my mind! Most of the time, everyone else is thinking about what the plan might look like. In preparation for our meetings, many have brought plans from other campuses that they are excited to share. Sometimes I am asked to bring eight to 10 examples of plans so that the end game is apparent. No matter how many times I have tried to show teams options, they become immediately preoccupied with what is *in* the plans of other colleges!

After many years of word-smithing lengthy plans, I have come to believe that our best option in private higher education is a simple, one-page visual that helps to share key strategic components with stakeholders. We've mentioned that Credo uses the balanced scorecard business method for planning. Credo has also adapted this as the Thriving Scorecard for colleges and universities to best represent their unique perspectives and needs. The elements of a scorecard are represented on a strategy map, which allows us to see:

- Aspirational vision/mission
- Foundational values
- Strategic priorities
- Strategy (strategic objectives with causal links)

Strategy Map

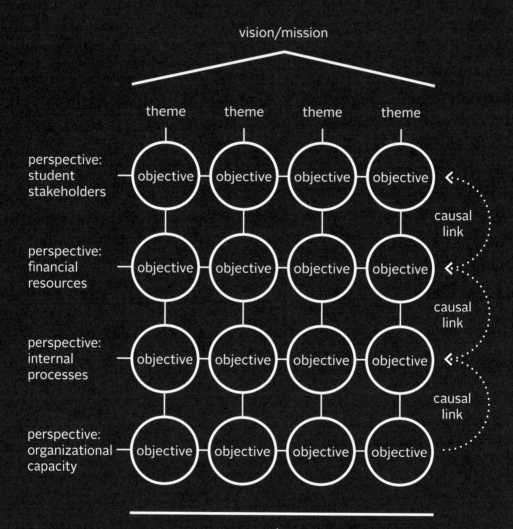

WHERE IS THE STRATEGY IN YOUR STRATEGIC PLAN?

Strategic plans are often more operational or even tactical than strategic (Rohm, 2008). In higher education, this is not all the fault of the leaders. Over the years, our accrediting agencies have tended to look for very long and detailed strategic planning documents that were expected to include almost everything. According to Porter, "Operational effectiveness and strategy are both essential to superior performance, which after all, is the primary goal of any enterprise, but they work in very different ways" (1996, p.61).

I am often asked about the difference between an operational plan and a strategic plan. An operational plan covers functional areas and their related details. A strategic plan should focus on what needs to change, and leading change becomes the focal point for college and university presidents. Leaders are beginning to rethink how to shape the future of their institutions and they have discovered that short-term plans and limited changes may not be sufficient to achieve success (Alfred, 2011).

THE NEW NORMAL

Even though we must deal with the issues above, there is a moment when we need to jump in and start. I am finding that it is most productive to do this by opening up planning to today's current realities. Our accrediting agencies, our constituencies, and our government are all calling for the following things that are a part of the new normal.

Clarity

Rick shared an all-too-familiar story with me about a prominent community leader who sat on the board of a prestigious liberal arts college. After two meetings, the board member was not clear about where the institution was going, what the priorities were, how initiatives would be achieved, or how the college was progressing. When Rick explained that many colleges and universities were like this, the board member was not happy with that level of ambiguity. After all, he was a busy individual taking his time to serve this college, and had higher expectations.

We have to do more work to clarify our key strategy components, not because of accreditation, but because everyone is asking for it. This includes board members, donors, faculty, staff, and enrolling families. Clarity used to be a hope. It is now a requirement, trumped only by having an excellent team in place to perpetuate it (Lencioni, 2012).

Alignment

One of the most difficult things to do within a planning process is to create alignment. More specifically, we always want to be sure that the planning at the institutional level is clearly aligned and linked to planning at all levels of the institution. We want to bring all past planning initiatives and plans to the table so they can be integrated and aligned with the institutional strategic plan. For example, the goals of the admissions office need to point upward toward the goals of the institution; if there is a technology plan, it should clearly align with the institution's themes for the future.

Lencioni (2012) highlights that alignment is an extension of developing clarity, both of which are challenging work:

The second requirement for building a healthy organization—creating clarity—is all about achieving alignment. This is a word that is used incessantly by leaders, consultants, and organizational theorists, and yet for all the attention it gets, real alignment remains frustratingly rare. (p.73)

However, developing organizational clarity and alignment allows us to move ahead with greater purpose, unity, and effectiveness. We don't have to agree on everything, but the board, administration, faculty, and staff benefit from a clear sense of the general direction of the institution (Friedman, 2013).

Agility

Colleges and universities are big ships that do not turn quickly and are at real risk when they are around rocky shores! In this unprecedented era in higher education, institutions are facing high rates of change that require new levels of agility. Plans need to be living! We need to be ready to capture projects and initiatives that line up with vision, and implement them in new ways.

In a published report entitled *Disrupting College*, a leading researcher and his team write about emerging disruptive innovation and the opportunities to rethink old assumptions about higher education processes, places, and goals (Christiansen, Horn, Caldera, & Soares, 2011). Increasingly, college and university leaders need to engage new processes that allow for higher rates of effective change. We need to create an environment that allows innovation to come to the surface, model it for institutional effectiveness, and act on it with urgency.

Transparency

There have never been more calls for transparency in higher education. The White House website lists transparency as one of four priorities and reports that:

In the vein of transparency and accountability, President
Barack Obama tasked his administration with giving students
and families new tools and relevant information that will help
them make sound financial decisions in pursuing their higher
education goals. (2013, para.12, www.whitehouse.gov/issues/
education/higher-education)

Plans not only have to be written, they have to be executed with
greater visibility. This transparency extends itself to the progress of
strategic themes and objectives. There must be a way for each college
and university to efficiently show progress. It is becoming essential
to use tools that will make this easier and clearer.

There is an emotional toll when transparency is really in play.
The goals that we meet are celebrated, but those we don't meet are
now everyone's business. Both of these things are good.

Accountability

With greater clarity and transparency comes greater accountability.
We have seen the last of the days where we could slide by without
presenting clear progress and outcomes to our constituencies.
Conferences (Lederman, 2009), legislatures, and accreditors and even
the public are calling for greater accountability (Leveille, 2005).

These new directives about accountability are good for us. We
will learn to use metrics better, choose them better and define them
better. We will learn how to measure things we thought were not
measurable! I am also hoping that this charge will help us put and
keep the right people in the right seats. It will be clear when action is
not taking place, and corrections can be made.

Increased Revenue and Contained Costs

Although it might seem strange to include increased revenue and reduced expenses in the category of the new normal, it is necessary. We must hold ourselves accountable to the appropriate financial models and assessments that will allow the greatest efficiency and net revenue increases. Later we will talk more about the inability to embrace mission without a margin of revenue that allows people, spaces, and programs to thrive. There are numerous entitlements in higher education. For a long time we have done our business without good processes and systems that put students at the center. When we are able to schedule classes and collect money with students at the center instead of faculty and staff, we will have taken a huge step forward.

ASKING THE RIGHT QUESTIONS

The new normal is also demanding that we answer the right questions. These questions are what help shape our strategy maps:

1. Where are we going? (Aspirational Vision/Mission)
2. Why do we do what we do? (Foundational Values)
3. What is our value proposition to our stakeholders? (Stakeholders)
4. Which strategic priorities? (Strategic Themes)
5. How are we going to get there, and how are we progressing? (Strategic Objectives, Meaningful Measures)
6. Who is responsible for what? (Owners)
7. When are we going to do what? (Initiatives, Projects)

SHOULD WE SWAT THE SWOT?

When I first announced to our team and Rick that I never wanted to do another SWOT analysis, eyes opened wide! Someone said, "I'm not sure you should try to undo 50 years of SWOT analysis history!"

But I am determined to push us all in another direction as we embrace this new environment of higher education and the urgency that comes along with it. After hundreds of SWOT analyses, I am highly skeptical about the ability of the exercise to promote our most strategic thinking. I realize that a piece of this comes from our own need to identify gaps and fix them, but the plight we are facing in private higher education today dictates a more focused look at how we might move ahead.

Obsessive contemplation about what is strong, what is weak, what is a threat, and what is an opportunity can bring misleading and irrelevant information to the table, especially if the campus community has been insulated. At the very best, it is an accumulation of the ideas of a very busy and somewhat isolated community of educators who are hungry for some answers to the dilemmas of this era.

I am suggesting that we start in a different place. At Credo, we use three tools to help the leadership of the college prepare for planning:

1. We ask the leadership teams of each of our clients to complete an online inventory based upon the nine elements of thriving colleges in this book. The survey is used to determine the urgency of certain areas on that particular campus, and the consistency of leadership and planning team responses.

2. We present the aggregate results of the survey and ask the leadership and planning teams to respond to the evident gaps and opportunities possible in their culture.

3. We bring the current external threats to higher education to the table with information that will be helpful in determining strategies that meet the challenges.

In other words, we believe that in order to move from surviving to thriving, the necessary actions are based around the nine elements in the Thriving Framework. Distraction and preoccupation with personal agenda initiatives and traditional methodologies will make strategic points of action less likely to emerge. It is important for every college to place their focus on themes and projects that will make the most difference in sustainability for the future.

DISCUSSION QUESTIONS:

CULTURE OF PLANNING & INNOVATION

- Do you have a current strategic plan?
- Was it created in the last three years?
- Was the strategic planning process collaborative?
- Is there a clear accountability system with timetables that makes the strategic plan implementable?
- Is there a dashboard of key indicators that would allow you to know that the strategic plan has been implemented?
- Is there campus-wide knowledge of the strategic plan?
- Is the plan a shared vision among campus constituencies?
- Does the plan include a mission and vision statement?
- Is the plan aligned with your budgeting process?
- Are your strategic objectives clearly measurable?
- Is there an annual strategic planning process by divisions or departments that is closely tied to your institutional strategic initiatives?
- Are your institutional strategic initiatives largely operational in nature?
- Are there any game-changers in your institutional strategic initiatives?

Chapter 8

Net Revenue & Strategic Finance

The first of several calls came in early September: "We didn't make our goal!" As I asked questions, I sensed an element of surprise in that statement – the institution was not prepared for that outcome. Digging even deeper, I came to understand that the goal was set at an enrollment number never before achieved. Next, I heard, "We did not make our annual fund goal either." I learned that the annual goal was set higher than ever before, and it was essential for it to be reached in order to meet the annual budget. Again, there appears to be an element of surprise. The next step was to cut the budget. September had turned into a dreaded month on this and many other campuses. With all of the celebration and excitement at the beginning of an academic year, these negative surprises drain energy and institutional self-esteem before the fall semester is even well underway.

Thriving institutions understand that the execution of their mission and vision is dependent upon the financial health of the institution. They budget conservatively, and almost never on a goal that has not been met in the past. They use leading indicators so there are no surprises. Their finances are always connected with their strategy, corrections to their strategies are being executed monthly, and adjustments are being made (Chabotar, 2006). The opening of the school year is never about a mystery. It should always be about a successful journey.

In higher education, we have been the champions of lagging indicators. Our metrics almost always reflect end-of-semester or end-of-academic-year goals. In order to be accountable and responsible in the future, we will need to get better at setting forward-looking monthly goals, and understanding what needs to be done if they are not met.

Most private colleges will be perpetually tuition-driven (Hunter, 2012). We will always need to keep a watchful eye on the factors that lead to discrepancies in our enrollment successes. For

Simply put, if there is no margin, then there is no mission!

that reason, recruiting and retention must be at the center of our strategic planning so that students can be at the center of our mission. Simply put, if there is no margin, then there is no mission!

$$margin = revenue - expenses$$

Sometimes we are fooled because we refer to our colleges and universities as nonprofits. Don't be fooled! We still need three to five percent in reserve each year to reinvest in new programs, new faculty, and new facilities. We need to be very careful when debt grows to over 50% of our operating revenue, or when our endowment is less than our annual budget. The KPMG Composite Financial Index (CFI) and the Department of Education's Test of Financial Strength (TFS) remind us that being in the black is not enough. A CFI score below 3.0, and/or a TFS score below 1.5 tells us that we need more margin/net revenue (Hunter, 2012). We need net revenue to have sound financial health. This means that every year we have to generate new revenue, and not just by raising tuition. We also need to make cuts each year so we have funds to do the new and creative things we need to do.

TO GROW OR NOT TO GROW: IS IT OPTIONAL?

Unless a college or university endowment is strong enough to fulfill the obligations of scholarships necessary to meet enrollment goals, growth is not optional, it is essential. Growth for growth's sake is not enough, though. The key here is strategic growth (Keller, 1983, 2004). It is all about how you will cut the pie! Which constituencies should grow?

When I speak to faculty and staff at our client institutions about necessary growth, I often see raised eyebrows and the onset of skepticism. This is not a blanket recommendation that looks the same for every campus – it is up to each institution to understand where growth should occur. When I say it is about how to cut the pie, I mean it. There must be conscious decisions about how many graduate students, how many traditional undergraduate students, how many nontraditional degree-completion students, etc., so that we are planning for growth, not responding to it, or to the lack of it.

Without careful planning, the pie will cut itself. All of a sudden a college or university will find itself with more nontraditional students than it wanted, or it will find that its discount rate has climbed to an untenable place because the pie was not cut properly, and there are too many students with too many needs. This is all about taking control of your own destiny. It is about intentional planning instead of a reactionary response. Evidence is clear that solid planning makes the difference for the future. Planning for growth can change the very nature of the conversations within the organization. (Bryson, 2011).

If growth is non-negotiable, and in most places it is, then I encourage college leaders to study it carefully. Financial models about growth are essential, and should be shared so decisions are credible and understood. Both Chabotar (2006) and Townsley (2009) offer information on building sound models. Endless discussion and conflict should not impede growth and the strategies needed to make it happen. It is extremely important to make these decisions, then implement them immediately. Some of these decisions are difficult, and therefore they are often delayed to avoid controversy. This scenario caps institutional progress and halts the journey to thriving.

ADMISSIONS: A WHOLE NEW WORLD

Whether you are admitting students from a large pool of applications and have the luxury of *building* and *shaping* your classes, or you are *gathering* your classes by recruiting as many students as you can from your applicant pool, it is all very different than it was just 10 years ago.

Hoover and Supiano (2013) report that enrollment teams are facing unprecedented disruption from past practices and predictability.

I can remember my days as chief admissions officer at Elon University with great specificity. I remember that if I could determine the right number of names to buy at the top of the funnel, and I could achieve certain conversion rates on inquiries, visits, applications, and acceptances, I could easily predict the number of students that would enroll. We used to be able to just gather our students for the class. Those days are gone. Prospective students today can move all the way to the bottom of our funnel and know everything about us, without us knowing they exist! They use the Facebook page or the website to study the college or university. They know us, and then they contact us, not the other way around. Everything is upside down. It is because of this change that we have surprises. It is no longer possible for us to control the journey of a large number of students without innovative and intentional strategies that give us more control and fewer surprises.

On the next page, you will see a diagram of an admissions funnel. You will notice that along the sides of the funnel there are still students who flow through it in the traditional ways. But inside the funnel, there are pipelines that allow us to predict our outcomes more efficiently. Now we are recruiting by building the class with intentionality. Pipelines are vehicles that bring prospective students to the edge of campus. They can be a geographic area, an academic program, a co-curricular program, an experience, or a constituency, but all pipelines have four things in common:

1. They have a champion.
2. They have a goal.

Admission Building Pipeline

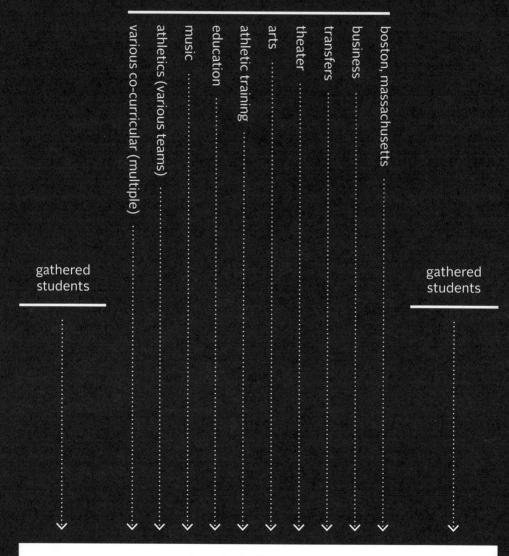

built
students

various co-curricular (multiple)

athletics (various teams)

music

education

athletic training

arts

theater

transfers

business

boston, massachusetts

gathered
students

gathered
students

gathered + built = new class

3. They have a source of specific names.
4. They have a business plan.

Athletics is the clearest example of how a pipeline works (Peale, 2013). A coach will find a student based on his or her connections in the athletic world. The business plan consists of the travel budget, high schools, and coach connections that will come into play that year. The goal for their annual roster is clear, and they champion their students through the funnel until enrollment is complete.

We also have clear examples of common pipelines in nursing, music, and transfers (Hoover, 2010). It is also possible to have a pipeline identified as Boston, Massachusetts. That means there is a serious alum and counselor working together for a goal with an intentional business plan, and a specific source of names and relationships.

Pipelines can have goals of 100 or goals of five. When the four crucial points are in order, there is less chance for a surprise in September. The funnel is under better control. We refer to these prospective students as *leveraged* students. They are getting a more personal and deliberate push down the funnel. They also retain better because of these relationships.

There are many colleges still attempting to work the funnel in traditional ways. I don't believe this will serve us well in the future. Our students have too many choices, and they are looking for a way to join our communities with already established special connections. When we have done a great job of building the class, then we can talk about shaping the class. That high-level strategy would only be implemented if a college or university sees three to four consecutive years of increased traditional undergraduate enrollment. Shaping the class would mean being able to decline some applicants from the least qualified group of students, and limiting aid to shape net revenue in a positive way.

I would be remiss if I led you to believe that most prospective students know what they would like to major in. In fact, it is probably not smart for us to ask that question. We know that the majority of students are unclear about their major (Simon, 2012). That fact alone should tell us that marketable and appealing pipelines are necessary to draw them to us, and good teaching is necessary to help them find their way to specific majors as their journey continues.

Although there are multiple innovative strategies now to enhance enrollment numbers, the overall philosophy of pipelines will be crucial to the future of our revenue issues. Every private college will need to be deliberate about identifying these distinct ways that they can attract students to their experience.

Conservative budgeting takes place in the office of our chief financial officers, but it lacks legs if it is not complemented by a predictable admissions strategy that will protect the college or university from the September frenzy and disappointment.

RETENTION: KEEP THEM ONCE WE HAVE THEM!

The average cost of recruiting a student in 2011 for private colleges was over $2,000, and may soon be over $3,000 (Pullaro, 2012). If we are putting that much effort into bringing those students into our communities, we have to get better at keeping them!

Many have documented the financial value of retention (Bean, 1990). To the right, you'll see a chart of what can happen to net revenue with small increases in retention. It is not work for the faint of heart! It demands a comprehensive solution, and a change

New Net Revenue Impact

Improving Fall-to-Fall
Retention: New Net
Revenue Impact

350
First-time Freshman

$15,000
Net Tuition

70% — Current Fall-to-Fall FF Retention

71% — **$52,500**
Moves from 70% to 71% for one year

71% + **71%** + **71%** — **$279,000**
Maintained at 71% for three years

73% + **73%** + **73%** — **$838,000**
Maintained at 73% for three years

75% + **75%** + **75%** — **$1,397,000**
Maintained at 75% for three years

Based on Tuition Revenue Only

in the way we have thought for many years. Students have many options, and they are conscious of them at all times. If a problem occurs, they always have a plan B or C to turn to. It is our job to keep them from getting to that place. The strategies for increasing retention percentages will demand courageous leadership, and the commitment to educate faculty and staff about the issues that need to be addressed for student success.

FUNDRAISING: A SYSTEM, NOT A PERSON!

Although we know that tuition will drive the net revenue, fundraising is essential for the project work that we need to do both programmatically and in capital initiatives. It is also essential because the annual fund is so crucial to the budget. This is another place where I have seen budgeting that is not conservative. In fact, it is not unusual for a budget to be built and a determination made that the annual fund will make up the difference, even if that amount has never been raised before.

I don't think I've been at a single one of the 200 schools with which I've consulted where I've heard that the fundraising system has been running beautifully for numbers of years. It seems like we all woke up to the intricacies of fundraising strategy about 20 years ago. We had been doing an awful lot of friend-raising, but it wasn't resulting in the kind of revenue that we needed to attack the projects that were essential to our success. I know that many of the elite and selective institutions were ahead of the game, but there was and is much work to be done in most of our private colleges to bring us to a level where fundraising can contribute effectively to our strategic initiatives.

Too often, much of the time in development/advancement offices is spent on smaller gifts. There is always difficulty identifying those who can make the most difference, and small staffs make it almost impossible to act on every lead we identify.

All of this is compounded by how personality-centered our fundraising programs are. Thriving colleges have implemented a system to be sure that there is continuity in relationships and proposals. The system is not dependent upon a person. Until colleges and universities take a step toward putting these systems in place, they will be susceptible to inconsistent stops and starts (Lanning, 2007). Donor loss is always present in these circumstances.

Leaders in this area are difficult to find (Lanning, 2007). They have to have a rare combination of strategy, communication skills, relationship skills, and the ability to close an ask. They are often seen with skepticism if they do not have a long-term tie to the institution, so it is troubling to see *The Chronicle of Philanthropy* report the average length of service for fundraisers at 16 months, with an average turnover cost of over $125,000 (Flandez, 2012).

It is comforting to me, and I hope to our college presidents, that the skill set for fundraising can be customized. Everyone fundraises using his or her own special set of strengths. I see more and more college leaders moving to hiring relationally-connected fundraisers. They find it easier to secure coaching and training than to search for someone that will not be committed to the long-term vision. I love thinking about raising money as a way to provide opportunities for people to feel good about themselves. If a president can find the heart of a donor, the plan unfolds without much difficulty. It's all about believing in something so passionately that you cannot resist asking for help!

The Gates Foundation and other philanthropy groups continue to reshape both higher education and fundraising (Young, 2012). As we've mentioned, donors like the Gates and others are serving in the role of venture philanthropists who want to see a clear return on their investment (Saltman, 2010). In most cases, it is a social return rather than a financial return on investment that they are after. That said, donors increasingly want to see clear vision, strategy, and accountability of progress for the funds they contribute. Those who rely on older methods of fundraising may find themselves being passed up by institutions who are willing and able to provide more clarity on their projects and progress.

VIABLE ALTERNATIVE REVENUE STREAMS

When I look at the challenges of many of our small private institutions, and see the discount rates they are struggling to lower, it is difficult to understand how they will survive without embracing one or more alternative revenue streams. The two biggest players in this arena are adult and online education. We must not see these new territories as threatening and negative, but instead as opportunities to make a difference for the learners we serve while preserving the undergraduate traditions we've come to love. We must be brave enough to embrace them!

Adult Education

When we talk about alternative tuition revenue streams, the most effective one is adult education. There have been many other suggestions and options that fall short of their original promise. Retirement homes, daycare centers, and bookstores just don't make it! The reason I am partial to expanding revenue streams in the area of adult education is because I believe so strongly in the distinct missions of private colleges and universities, and know that when discount rates are growing, there *must* be a mission-based expansion of constituencies so that financial health is possible. I am also aware that there are millions of adult students in our country, and in other countries, who need education to make a difference in their lives. It is our responsibility to open these doors, and a necessity to expand the impact of our passion so we can continue to serve students of all ages well.

We in higher education did ourselves a strong disservice in early discussions about adult education. In many places, it was seen as a cash cow, but we were shortsighted in our vision about what this extension of mission could mean. If we truly believe that education will solve many of the problems precipitated by ignorance, we have to understand our role in process. The fact that these programs bring an alternative revenue stream to the table is important, but should not be at the center of their significance.

Once a college or university is convinced to move ahead in the realm of adult education, the confusion is mind-boggling. There are all kinds of decisions to be made, and they are not easy. The first decision that most colleges and universities must address is whether they will go at this endeavor alone or with a partner. Embracing a partner is definitely easier. Leadership, marketing expertise, and manpower are the essential ingredients that these for-profit partners deliver. The downside is giving up a share of the revenue.

The key to this initial decision is about leadership. Private colleges and universities can implement these programs without partners, but not without entrepreneurial and innovative leaders.

These positions are difficult to fill. The skill set of those who can make this happen consists of a blend between solid business savvy and passionate educational goals. It's fair to say that we have seen many of these programs implemented without clear leadership, and without the academic quality and technological sophistication needed to match their traditional undergraduate counterparts. That is difficult for faculty, and tends to fracture their loyalty to the program.

This area must be addressed with a careful blend of urgency, integrity, quality, and depth. The question is, how will you do it? Models need to be carefully designed. Experts need to be hired to develop and implement these programs. Faculty need to be trained and encouraged to step forward in the process. Careful evaluation should be extended to all partnerships in this area so that long-term mistakes are not made. The wonderful thing is that we have an opportunity to make a difference for adult learners and preserve the undergraduate traditions we've come to love. We must be brave enough to embrace it.

Online Education

More than ever, we are seeing online classes and programs as a clear option for those who want degrees. As leaders in higher education, it is our responsibility to embrace this world of new technology and make an attempt to provide programs that don't cheapen, but deepen, the online experience. It will be essential to address it in both the traditional and the nontraditional student worlds.

The colleges and universities who have embraced online classes for their own traditional-age students have done so with a great deal of creativity. An audit in the registrar's office has led these colleges to understand which classes their students are taking at other colleges and universities over the summer. With that information in hand, they are designing summer online programs to meet those needs. They are reclaiming their students over the summer. This allows selected faculty members to learn the skill of designing and delivering the classes, and gives students an option to stay at their own college for the summer but be in their hometown. Pricing on these classes must be lower and often they will meet in person before they leave the campus and when they return – a very creative option! It will be unusual for any 18-year-old student to go through life without taking an online class. It is our responsibility to prepare them for this.

The options for nontraditional age students abound! In fact, there are so many innovative ways to offer online programs and courses that it really does leave the door open for colleges and universities to be distinctive in this market, but is not an option to be hesitant once the decision is made to embrace it. The competition is moving quickly with an appropriate eye toward convenience and quality for adult students. Studies are proving that the outcomes of these programs are surpassing some more traditional methods (Means, Toyama, Murphy, Bakia & Jones, 2010). This is not something to be ignored, and is clearly not a delivery method without merit.

ACADEMIC EFFICIENCY: THE LAST FRONTIER!

When we talk about the efficient stewardship of funds, the last frontier is truly in the area of academic efficiency. It is the one place that we have been hesitant to dive in, and yet, there is a strong likelihood of waste and inefficiencies here. It has been our habit to be primarily faculty-centered when it comes to schedules and academic programs. I know this will be a controversial section, but it shouldn't be – I have always done what I do in admissions, fundraising, and strategic planning because I believe so much in what the faculty does. Learning will always be at the center in the heart of private higher education. My own private higher education in the liberal arts changed my life, but I am smart enough to know that we can do it all more efficiently.

Examining academic efficiency allows us to maximize our space, faculty time, class scheduling, and student engagement, leading to a reduction in expenditures and a streamlining of related processes. I have seen with my own eyes what it means to re-engineer and reshape a class schedule with the class-section caps in appropriate places, and the times centered around students. I've been privileged to watch processes that have saved forty to a hundred thousand dollars per year by reworking the schedule.

I'm also aware that there are academic programs, both majors and minors, in most colleges and universities that are there are because one person has been the champion. This is a positive practice, but only if those programs are drawing students and/ or contributing to the core curriculum in significant ways. We have been neglectful at setting the metrics necessary for deleting and adding academic programs. Without those systems in place, everything is personal, and can be troublesome when the person at the core of that cult of personality transitions away.

When programs are not a strong part of the central core curriculum, they must be reviewed frequently for their effectiveness and market value. Prospective students are looking for an experience, and that experience will lead them to a professor that they love and a major that they will someday embrace. Finding that major doesn't usually happen at the college fair table, but when admissions counselors are asked about a specific program frequently, it should be a high level indication to us that the program should be reviewed as an area of growth and increased marketing. The admissions office is a crucial place to ask about what programs we should be adding. Some programs are hot, and we need to use them as pipelines to populate all of our liberal arts programs! More than half of college freshmen today will change their majors, and even more are unsure about the majors they have chosen (Simon, 2012). It is essential to first capture their hearts and then refine their specific interests.

The other opportunity for examination of academic efficiency lies in academic organization. Whether the choice is to function as schools or as departments, there is need for a pragmatic element, generally at the administrative level, to protect learning from growing stale and ineffective. It is often true that there is too much academic organization in very small colleges, and too little of it in colleges that are growing. The art of designing the most appropriate and effective academic organization is an important one.

Before faculty members boot me out on this one, let me be very clear on this crucial point: while the academic program might be a spot to recapture funds through lean and efficient thinking, those funds *must* be reinvested in the academic program. There is so much that we can do to increase innovation and excitement for learning, but we are always short of funds. Those dollars can be uncovered through honing our academic efficiency, and reinvested back into learning. It is what thriving colleges and universities do!

YOUR CFO AS A PARTNER

A smart, innovative, and communicative chief financial officer is critical at private colleges and universities for net revenue and strategic finance to thrive. When that person is in place, there is much that can be accomplished. When I asked good CFOs what would be helpful to them in presidential behavior, this is what I heard:

- Be sure there is a budget calendar showing timelines for important budget due dates and final approval.
- Support holding budget guidelines equally across departments.
- Ask for financial models supported by data when every proposal for a new initiative is brought forward.
- Believe your CFO. If the CFO is not capable of being believed, find another one who can. If you refuse to believe a credible CFO, you will not succeed.
- Developing financial strength is everybody's work.

LINKING PLANNING AND FUNDING

Strategic planning has been at the heart of my work over the last 15 years. I have to admit that the process of getting colleges and universities on the same page to address strategic needs has been difficult, so much so that I needed a simple way to put their funding worries to rest in order to continue the planning. It is always going to be important to model funding issues for each strategic initiative, but the initial concerns about funding are frequently so intense that the innovation process can be frozen.

As I have many times over the last 15 years, I turned to my friend and colleague Dr. Gerry Francis at Elon University. I asked him to give me a simple way to address funding of strategic initiatives, and give it an important place in the discussion without inhibiting the process. We decided to take a first step during the planning process by identifying, in general, where funds could be found. This step is key to move through the process, and give a clear understanding of reality to faculty and staff without bogging them down in the specifics. The second step involves the more granular planning and prediction of expense and revenue, and requires the financial modeling necessary to set final goals.

To begin, look at each of the goals in a plan and link it with a funding source in general terms. Gerry and I chose six categories and have used them successfully to this day. There are limited places to find funding in a college budget, and the sources include:

1. Surplus revenue generated by growth.
2. Borrowing.
3. Interest from endowment.
4. Fundraising.
5. Partnership initiatives.
6. Money available by concluding another initiative and taking it out of the budget.

It is an interesting activity for planning teams to take each of their goals or initiatives and identify one of these categories for funding them. Reality sets in! When it is pretty clear that there will be no initiative unless there is growth, there is a sense of unity around growing. When the facts are known about the borrowing history of the institution, then the possibilities or non-possibilities become very evident. A history of fundraising is a wake-up call for those who believe that every project can be funded by a donor, and most campus communities are shocked by the small amount of endowment interest that can be used as a contribution to scholarship funding.

The newest of the categories is partnership initiatives. We are seeing more and more proposals for partnerships with local communities and statewide organizations. It is still too early to understand what is going to happen with mergers and acquisitions in the higher education industry. I've been a part of the discussions between colleges that have an interest in this, and so far there are many obstacles. With the right amount of attention, though, it is going to be exciting to watch how colleges and their cities and towns come together for good.

> If we don't start aligning plans with budget and funding, we will continue to make beautiful plans without beautiful outcomes!

The most troublesome category is the one that includes stopping something to start something. Adding and deleting program and budget items is one of the most difficult undertakings, so it is also where collaboration in the budgeting process is essential. The financial models needed to make these decisions are still infrequent on campuses. This is the category that usually brings criticism to administration when it isn't handled correctly.

I have also designated a special category for initiatives that do not need funding but demand *focus*. When it is determined that focus on a strategic objective is what's needed, rather than a dollar allocation, it becomes imperative to put someone in charge of that objective and adjust his or her responsibilities to allow achievement of that objective.

Categorizing goals and initiatives gives a sense of control to planning teams, though the detail needed later in the process is a more difficult endeavor. The bottom line is that if we don't start aligning plans with budget and funding, we will continue to make beautiful plans without beautiful outcomes!

THE VALUE PROPOSITION/SCHOLARSHIP DILEMMA

The days are over for private colleges to claim that they have a distinction around warmth and personal attention. Every college has used that value proposition over time, and it doesn't connect to the investment that we are requesting. We must get better at showing students and their families why we are a preferred choice. Every prospective student needs to have a strong feeling of belonging when they are making a college choice.

Recently I have been talking about value propositions, plural, because I don't know of one college or university that is not recruiting groups of students with individual needs and interests. For example, do you believe that an athlete might be more influenced by a value proposition designed specifically for him or her? Do you believe that a student from Massachusetts would value hearing about the college experience from another student from Massachusetts? When we are recruiting classes of less than 500, it is essential for us to begin to segment our recruiting pool,

> Strengthening your value proposition and generating more net revenue is better than just cutting costs or being cheaper.

and address them with the value proposition that will encourage the investment necessary to join our community. When the value proposition is strong, then the financial sacrifice is worth it! Additionally, endless research tells us that strong organizations always put adding value (better) over cutting costs (cheaper). In other words, strengthening your value proposition and generating more net revenue is better than just cutting costs or being cheaper. (Raynor & Ahmed, 2013).

Why is your institution distinctive? Bold thinking must take place for your value proposition to sparkle and shine. Many college administrators will tell me that they are going to increase their numbers of internships because that is what parents want. That is true, and can be a great part of value proposition, but the bold thinkers are requiring internships and using dual transcripts to record them! It is time stop counting the obstacles to innovation and to start acting. If we are going to preserve the essence of the private colleges that we love, we will need to polish it and make it shine. It is a huge sacrifice for parents to offer this gift to their children. We need to prove that it is worth it.

When the value proposition is clear, then applications increase. When applications increase, we have the ability to shape financial aid packages in ways that will increase net revenue. We will also need to embrace the most credible, reliable financial aid leveraging strategies available. The two of these things combined can make a difference in net revenue that will change the trajectory of the future.

We cannot discuss net revenue and finance without addressing that troublesome issue of *tuition discounting*, and even though I have written it, I would prefer to never use the term again. The discussion about it consumes hours and hours of staff and board of trustee attention. Discounting tuition, through extensive scholarship policies designed to attract students, means a direct loss to the budget lines that we need so desperately to address the elements of thriving colleges and universities in this book. I would much rather discuss net revenue and the ways that we can increase it.

I was fortunate enough to understand my responsibility to enrollment in a place that did not embark on the tuition-discount journey. Elon University always lifted the value proposition higher than the scholarship proposition. That meant developing and designing a value proposition that would be attractive to a specific constituency of active and energized students. What a gift it was to begin my admissions career understanding that philosophy, and what a joy to see what those funds could do to contribute to a thriving institution!

I know that colleges and universities would love to roll back the clock and have that foresight. I also know that consistent leadership in many of our colleges and universities would have made that more possible, but we are where we are, and the solution to this scholarship dilemma is a difficult one to identify. Buying students with scholarships will never be the long-term answer, and buying better students at high scholarship levels will not be the answer.

The solution is different in each institution, but essentially it includes a determination that step by step, the programs and distinctions and experiences *must* get better for the scholarship offers to be decreased. Every institution should recruit and appropriately scholarship the best students they can afford, and teach them well! The sacrifice needed to afford a private school education *must* be worth it to the families we serve.

SUMMARY

We want to push to college and university presidents to be bolder in addressing these issues around net revenue and finance. It would be wonderful if every college leader could leave a legacy that was compelling and significant when they retire or move to another campus. This will be impossible until we have addressed the issues of financial stability. Right now, that is defining our presidents. When it is tackled with success, then the other legacies can come alive!

DISCUSSION QUESTIONS:
NET REVENUE & STRATEGIC FINANCE

- Are you budgeting conservatively to ensure surplus funds annually?
- Are you budgeting on a proven and realistic enrollment goal?
- Is there a specific enrollment management plan designed to meet all enrollment goals?
- Are there specific net revenue goals in each new student enrollment revenue stream (e.g. undergraduate traditional students, graduate students, adult degree-seeking students, etc.)?
- Are you consistently meeting your net revenue goals in each of the new student enrollment revenue areas?
- At each stage of the admissions funnel (inquiry, application, accepted, enrolled) and in each of the enrollment new student revenue areas, are you consistently raising conversion rates?
- Are you using predictive modeling as a part of your admissions strategy?
- Do your conversion rates for prospective students who visit attest to the fact that they have had a WOW experience?
- Are there specific net revenue goals for the retention of students at the institution?
- Do you have a strategic financial aid leveraging plan that includes both merit and need-based aid?
- Is the financial aid leveraging plan helping you to meet your enrollment AND your net revenue goals?
- Have you made cuts in your admissions budget over the last three years?

- Have you established any alternative (innovative and entrepreneurial) revenue streams?
- Is your advancement team spending the majority of its time on annual fund and unrestricted gifts under $250?
- Is there a regularly scheduled moves management meeting for the president to assure strategic visits and asks?
- Is there a specific metric that measures the activity and productivity of advancement officers?
- Are your annual fund goals set specifically to make up gaps in the institutional budget?
- Are you actively engaged in securing planned and deferred gifts for the institution?
- Is there a cultivation society resulting in increased gifts of $1,000 or more?
- Is your advancement staff primarily made up of experienced development professionals?
- Has the advancement office budget been cut at any point over the last three years?
- Is there a strong and compelling case for support at the institution?
- Have you had a capital campaign during the last five years?
- Is the majority of the fundraising done at your institution for the purpose of meeting budget shortfalls?
- Are 100% of your board of trustees members supporting the institution at an appropriate level, according to their capacity?
- Is your donor prospect pool growing on an annual basis?

Chapter 9

Student Learning
& Success

I am standing on a campus talking to the provost and the vice president for admissions, and we are talking about the enrollment number for fall semester. At first, I love the conversation! It is a fall day, and I love being on campuses during the fall. Students have that enthusiasm we always see when they are getting to know each other, settling into new classes, and building new relationships with their professors.

It is almost perfect, but the conversation takes an all-to-familiar turn. The provost says, "Since we didn't meet our retention goals this year, we'll need to increase the admissions goal." My heart sinks. They're going to take the easy way out! Instead of looking at a comprehensive solution to retaining students, which will encourage everyone and support the core of their mission, they will try to solve this problem in admissions again! What will it take to bite this bullet?

College presidents must be courageous enough to embrace the means to true student success if we really wish to have distinctive and authentic value propositions. This issue is not just about increasing a retention percentage or improving customer service. Student learning and success is at the center of everything we believe in. When approached with intentionality and consistency, it will transform our students, and through them, the world.

Current trends, like *swirling students* who move to another college whenever they hit a bump in the road, present huge challenges to retention (Selingo, 2012). As educators, we believe deeply that students must attack and embrace the difficulties they face in life and learning. For this reason, we must take student success to the extreme and focus on retaining our students with a passion. The challenge to identify the issues and intervene with best practice is in front of us, and it will not go away. College presidents must invest in this journey. They must understand it and implement the comprehensive solutions necessary to make it better!

WHAT DOES STUDENT LEARNING AND SUCCESS MEAN?

Teach Well the Students You Have

When I am speaking publicly about the elements in this book, and I come to the section on student learning and success, I cannot wait for this part of the discussion. Teaching the students you have is at the very core of what it means to be an educator, and a true and positive focus on this should be central to all student success efforts on your campus. My passion for this probably has to do with my formal training in special education and exceptional children's programs. In all realms of life, I believe that we must meet people wherever they are and take them to a place of their highest potential!

There are thriving colleges all over this country with open-door access. They are successful because their programs, curricula, pedagogy, and support services are matched perfectly to the students they understand so well.

I clearly understand that teaching students with brilliant minds is rewarding, and I also understand that every teacher longs for that connective moment when what you have been trying to communicate lights up the eyes of a student. But I also know for a fact that the students we teach will make a difference in the world if we can meet them where they are, and transform their strengths into action.

> I know for a fact that the students we teach will make a difference in the world if we can meet them where they are, and transform their strengths into action.

These are today's students! They are prepared in different ways, are less resilient, and are "unable to summon strategies to cope" (Bips, 2010, para 2). They often have higher and more unrealistic expectations than the students of a decade ago. Levine and Dean call this "a generation on a tightrope" (2012). The art of designing a customized curriculum, program, and set of experiences for the students that you know belong to you is indeed a legacy-building story. If we would teach well the students that we have using proven, research-driven strategies, we would see student success climb beyond our wildest dreams (Habley, Bloom, & Robbins, 2012).

All students, regardless of their prior academic achievement or their socio-economic status, can thrive (Schreiner, Louis, & Nelson, 2012).

Learn their strengths, feed those strengths, and help them manage their weaknesses. Providing aspirational hope through this type of support can bring personal and academic transformation (Lopez, 2013). Pascarella and Terenzini's research (2005), three decades in the making, tell us that some college and university experiences are changing lives in compelling ways. Some of our most challenging students are running the largest companies in the world, receiving teacher-of-the-year awards, and ultimately making the most significant differences in mission and service. We have to meet them where they are when they come to us, and take them to someplace of wonderful significance.

What a bonus that our retention metrics will increase as we go, giving us more opportunity to invest in those students we love, and in our own teaching! Reinvesting in student learning can lead to so many high-impact initiatives for student success, such as advising interventions with selected student populations, developing a comprehensive learning assistance center, pre-enrollment financial aid counseling, summer orientations, peer mentoring, and more. Excellent definitions of these and other high-impact student success initiatives are readily available through ACT (2010). Through this cycle of investment and return, we will be assured of having more opportunity to help more students succeed in the decades to come.

A key part of that investment and return cycle is to publically share our stories of student success. We talked a great deal in the *Institutional Story* chapter about outcomes, and they are no less important to improving student success. These stories tell countless tales of students who came to our institutions not ready to embrace learning the way we wanted them to, but who, through nurturing and our carefully crafted student experiences, have gone on to great personal success. These stories have resoundingly happy endings!

The Successful Student

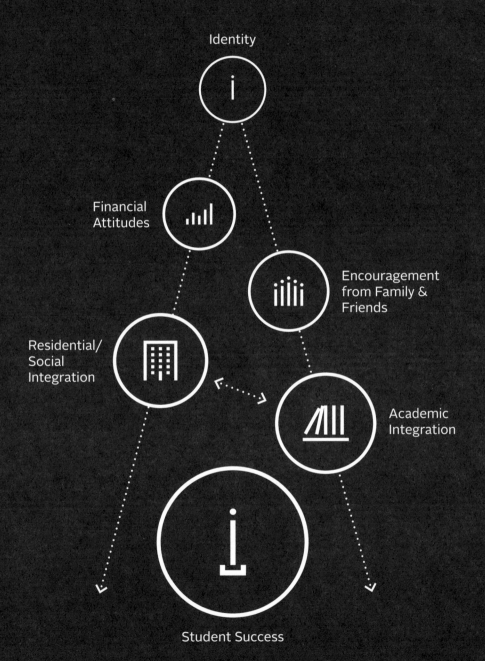

Identity

Financial Attitudes

Encouragement from Family & Friends

Residential/ Social Integration

Academic Integration

Student Success

Adapted from Cabrera, Nora, and Casteneda, 1993; Robbins, Allen, Peterson and Le, 2006.

THE "IT'S NOT US, IT'S THEM" MYTH

Sometimes we hear, "Doesn't our retention rate have more to do with the students in our incoming class than with how good our programs are? We've seen the research." When we look at differences in university retention and graduation rates, it's easy to look first at the academic profile of the incoming class and think that must be the only rational answer! Credo's lead consultant on student success, Dr. Joretta Nelson, weighs in passionately on this topic. The answer is yes... But no.

Dr. Joretta Nelson

I respond to this question as a student success scholar, a practicing student success consultant, and as an individual who spends a great deal of time synthesizing the most recent research related to improving conditions for student success.

Prior academic achievement is still the most reliable predictor of first-year retention and persistence to degree, particularly prior high school performance, high school quality, and high school curriculum (Robbins, 2006). To that end, there is a correlation between the admission standards of an institution and its retention/graduation rates. Institutions admitting larger percentages of students with higher prior academic achievement metrics will likely experience higher mean retention and graduation rates.

However, prior academic achievement only explains 25% of the variance in first-year achievement and retention to the second year (Robbins et al., 2003; 2006). Seventy-five percent of the variance is yet to be explained. The research of the last two decades has begun to fill this gap and is making progress. Psycho-social factors have been key areas of research and now help to explain an additional 5 – 15% of this variance, while controlling for prior academic achievement and socio-economic status (Pascarella & Terenzini, 2005; Robbins et al., 2006; Schreiner, 2012; 2013). In addition, a tremendous amount of research has been completed on different student groups (race/ethnicity, gender, first-generation), pointing toward substantive differences in performance and achievement in higher education, regardless of prior academic achievement (Pascarella et al., 2004; Schreiner, 2012; 2013).

What we are realizing is that increasing motivation, engagement, and support are strategies under the control of the institution through the educational environment created; prior academic achievement is not. The most recent research within the thriving-student framework points clearly to students who are able to thrive and succeed in all ways that institutions and constituents recognize as successful measures, in spite of prior academic achievement, socio-economic status, race/ethnicity, or first-generation status. Dr. Laurie Schreiner, Dr. Shane Lopez, Dr. Jenny Bloom, Dr. Wes Habley, Dr. Steve Robbins... the list goes on and on of those contributing to the most recent research about successful interventions – pointing to students out-performing their "prior picture." Such transformation is happening on different campuses (regardless of private/public or selectivity).

My point is that prior academic achievement gives us a window into one component of student readiness, and is a strong, validated predictor. However, prior academic achievement does not explain 75% of the variance in first-year student achievement and retention. This implies that what institutions have been doing to manage the 75% has not been effective – not that that 75% is not malleable. The "proof" is in the variance in retention and graduation rates within selectivity ranges in each segment of achievement ranks (ACT, 2012). With a swing of as much as 20% in the standard deviation within one selectivity range, it is apparent that different institutions provide different experiences and have different results. Thriving private institutions are placing student success at the center of their focus (Credo, 2012; Kuh et al., 2005). My concerns with a focus solely on prior academic achievement as a rationale for lower expectations are that this position:

- Explains away responsibility of those serving our students.
- Sets low expectations for students, which are then lived down to.
- Fails to incorporate the most recent research on psychosocial factors related to student success and their role, adding 5% – 15% to the variance in first year retention and achievement and persistence to graduation (Robbins et al., 2006; Schreiner et al., 2012; 2013).

- Works from a position of gaps rather than a position of strengths.
- Compares institutions, rather than students individually within the institution.
- Fails to incorporate recent empirical research on students of color, first-generation students, and other student groups who respond differently to institutional environments.
- Fails to respond to the decreasing number of high-achieving, "well-prepared" students available in higher education, perpetuating an environment that may result in declining new student enrollment numbers in the coming decades.

Improving student success requires the combined efforts of both the student and the institution. George Kuh, in writing about exceptional institutions in this regard, reminds us that students must invest meaningful and appropriate time and effort in the right activities that lead to positive outcomes (2005). At the same time, our institutions must allocate the resources and organize their learning opportunities so that the majority of their students participate in these meaningful activities. The leaders of our thriving colleges and universities will make this their goal: continuously improving both the quality and number of engaging opportunities *and* the percentage of students who participate in those opportunities.

INNOVATIVE TEACHING AND LEARNING

The word *learning* has taken the place of the word *academics* for me. After all these years of interaction with colleges and universities, I am convinced that the way we address learning must evolve. It simply does not take place solely in the classroom. An integrated, respectful, and proactive relationship between academic affairs and student affairs is crucial for today's students to learn and thrive. Whether on the soccer field, in a residence hall, or in a classroom, learning is different for this generation. Today's students are outside of the classroom 80% of the time. It is essential for us to utilize their residential and co-curricular experiences to continue their learning.

Making the whole campus a learning environment brings a true sense of community and commitment to the institution, encouraging and supporting "learning at any time" (Shushok, Henry, Blalock, & Sriram, 2009). We must change our campus environment from one of eating and sleeping to one of living and learning (Chickering & Gamson, 1987; Bonwell & Eison, 1991), and our resources and our rewards must align with it. I note in the chapter on *Net Revenue and Strategic Finance* that through attention placed on academic efficiency – rethinking schedules, class-size, and academic organization for the sake of freeing up revenue and cleaning up processes – that any revenue released in this process should be reinvested in student learning. Investment must come at all levels!

ACTIVE AND EXPERIENTIAL LEARNING

Active learning, appreciative learning, and individualized learning are current best practices that will help retain students and promote their successes. Sometimes called "high impact educational practices"

(Kuh, 2008), these are common terms now used by educators. The problem is that they seem to be defined differently in every setting. We'll try to create some common ground. In essence, six initiatives are really at the core of these types of experiential learning:

1. Study abroad/study away
2. Undergraduate research
3. Community service
4. Internships
5. Leadership opportunities
6. Service learning

Most college presidents do not have trouble embracing these initiatives. We all believe they are good for students, but the colleges thriving in this area have incorporated these initiatives into their curriculum, implemented strategies to ensure that the majority of students experience them, and embraced co-curricular transcripts as a way to record involvement and compel conversation with students. It takes an amazing amount of courageous leadership and strong partnerships to outline the difference between a scattering of experiential opportunities and a system through which all students can participate.

VALUE PROPOSITION IN A STUDENT SUCCESS CHAPTER?

Absolutely! We have to always remember that families are sacrificing significant resources for this learning experience. We must deliver it! We have to treat students and their families the way we would want to be treated if we were investing in this way. Student success is all about understanding what a student needs, when they need it, and how we deliver it. It is about proving to parents that we know our business, and surprising them by our readiness for implementation of the promise we have made to them. The success of our students and the service to them must be invaluable. Our sticker price and scholarship policies become insignificant when we have been deliberate about delivery.

There has never been more conversation about jobs than with this generation of students and their families. While the vast majority of parents see the value of a college education in general (Hoover, 2011), we know that mom and dad are both concerned about future jobs for their graduates (Jaschik, 2013). It is our responsibility to connect students to vocation and calling early and throughout their time on our campuses (Tankersly, 2013). We must make "getting a job" a meaningful part of their education and our value proposition. While data collection can be challenging, the days are over when we can shy away from this discussion of jobs (Basken, 2012). Accreditation agencies, state and federal governments, and others are compelling us to be accountable in these areas (Supiano, 2013). Once again, sharing outcomes becomes crucial in improving student success in this area.

SO WHAT MAKES A DIFFERENCE?

Put Someone in Charge!
The concept of student learning and success is now alive and well at almost every college or university. We no longer need to be convinced that it is important, but it continues to be a topic full of

misconceptions. Until we are willing to examine the elements of the problem, we will probably never solve it.

The first of these elements is the myth that it is better for a group of people to lead the charge toward better retention metrics and student success. Student success is clearly everyone's responsibility, but without accountability and the authority to rally the troops, it very quickly becomes no one's responsibility. For success to happen, someone has to be in charge (Kuh, 2005).

Although current practice is not to give this position a seat at the president's table, I believe we are not far away from that thinking. Each college president will have to find a way to be sure that the director of student success has the authority to make the decisions necessary for collaborative projects that will change metrics and increase retention. The director of student success should have a very specific skill set. It won't surprise you to read that this person needs to be a partnership builder, must be respected by faculty and staff, and must be able to create "a partnership between academic and student affairs" (Kuh, 2005, p. 306). The elements and initiatives needed to pull a comprehensive solution together are complex and integrated. The projects involve multiple departments and demand institutional affirmation. The director of student success must be able to build bridges, walk across them, and lead others to follow.

Know the Numbers!

Understanding the metrics in student success is a great start to a journey that could bring new net revenue and mission effectiveness to each college or university. You must know your numbers! It is important to know who is staying and why they are staying. We have to understand why students choose us. Where do they go when they leave? Freshman-to-sophomore-year retention numbers and four-year graduation numbers must be broken down by groups so it becomes clear where to put strategy in place.

Again, in this area, we come face-to-face with our current practice of embracing lagging indicators, in which we report retention and graduation rates at the end and at the beginning of the academic year. I long for the day that we become gurus of leading indicators, the monthly and semester figures that allow us to correct, intervene, and strategize about affecting the annual numbers. Who is at risk in the first nine weeks of the semester? How do we identify the students? Who continues to struggle with the financial obligations necessary to continue at college? Who is not connected to a group on campus? These metrics can and should be identified, tracked, and accounted for publically. This transparency can help us initiate projects and tasks that will change those numbers for the better.

SUMMARY

Student learning and success is a comprehensive proposition. It takes investment, innovation, integration, and the ability to break through traditions and meet students exactly where they are. It means being more intrusive, and requiring those things that we believe are crucial in student development and learning. It means putting academic and student support services in systems and physical places that make them available to all students without embarrassment. It means recognizing that the holistic experience of learning is important enough to look at it differently, and includes a commitment to put student learning at the center of everything that we do.

DISCUSSION QUESTIONS:

STUDENT LEARNING & SUCCESS

- Is student learning and success a high priority for the president?
- Is student learning and success a high priority for your leadership team?
- Is student learning and success a high priority for your board of trustees?
- Is there one person designated to lead and coordinate the retention efforts on campus?
- Does your faculty have a good grasp of accurate retention challenges in today's environment?
- Does your staff have a good working knowledge of retention challenges on campus?
- Is student success clearly defined on campus?
- Are student success metrics regularly shared?
- Is your student success plan comprehensive and inclusive of all areas of your institution?
- Do you pay close attention to how financial aid is used to retain students?
- Are your student services oriented toward the student and family as a customer?
- Do you ensure that the majority of your students have experiential learning opportunities within the first year of their enrollment?
- Do you have an integrated general education curriculum that supports students in making connections within learning and career pathways?

- Are your career preparation and readiness programming integrated into the curriculum and co-curriculum experiences?
- Do you demonstrate a commitment to innovative teaching and learning?
- Would students say the use of support services is something most students utilize?
- Do you believe that students would say it is easy to get the help that they need in academic support when they need it?
- Is academic advising perceived as a critical asset to student success?
- Do you support your academic advisors with appropriate early and ongoing training?
- Do your students say, for the most part, that they are satisfied with academic advising?
- Is there a strong partnership in program development between academic affairs and student affairs on campus?
- Is your residential experience more about living and learning than eating and sleeping?
- Do you regularly review your academic programs to measure their impact on recruitment and retention?
- Do you have a protocol for appropriately adding and deleting academic and co-curricular programs on campus?

Chapter 10

Transformative Environments

Sarah, a prospective student, and her mother entered campus.

"I'm not sure about this," Sarah said sharply.

Surprised, her mother asked, "Why?"

"It just doesn't feel right to me," said Sarah.

"But we haven't even been here 30 seconds!" said her mother, exasperated.

Sarah and her mother made their way to the old main building to meet the admissions staff. The space was cluttered, but the people were kind and helpful. They told her about the rich heritage of the school, and the faculty who took a personal interest in their students. In fact, an admissions counselor pointed them toward the education building, where they were able to meet one of the education faculty members. The only place to meet was in the faculty member's cramped office, but the professor seemed really smart and warm.

At the end of the visit, Sarah's mom asked her how she was feeling about the college. Sarah said the people were great, but she was still wondering whether she could get past her first impressions of the campus. In the end, Sarah chose another college to attend.

I have said so many times that if I could figure out what feeling this was that students get when they step on a campus, I would be the most sought after consultant in the country! The campus environment is such an important piece of the success of thriving colleges. It is also an area of incredible frustration for colleges fighting to survive. Parents and students are demanding an atmosphere that is attractive, well kept, inviting, and high-tech. It is not unusual for them to find spaces on our campuses that are less appealing than those at their high schools.

The purpose of this chapter is to go beyond looking at blueprints in our discussion of facilities and campus space. We should begin with higher-level conversations with our stakeholders, and if we do, then we have a greater likelihood of matching our facilities with our needs and opportunities.

A friend and presidential candidate called me a couple of weeks ago to discuss his candidacy at one of our client colleges. He wanted to know if he could make it really shine and turn it around. His question was very focused. It was about the obstacles that he would have to overcome to bring this college from surviving to thriving. Whenever I get asked that question these days, I mentally go through the nine elements in this book to see what will be the biggest challenge, and my thoughts always come back to the same thing. It is usually possible to change direction on most things and improve them, but the big issue will be the campus itself. If the deferred maintenance is high and the campus is not appealing, the opportunity to turn things around is bleak.

As the conversation about the cost of private higher education continues in America, we will be pressed to define our value proposition in many ways. The campus facility is the most visible! Although it's unfortunate that beautiful green grass can mean superior programs to many families, it often does. Thriving colleges take this very seriously, and are paying close attention to transformative environments. During Credo Strategy Days, college presidents ask us most consistently about the following issues and concerns:

- Aligning spaces and places with mission and vision.
- Curb appeal and first impressions.
- The campus visit and welcome experience.
- What to build, and what to renovate.
- The residence hall experience.
- What is new in educational facilities.

ALIGNING ENVIRONMENT WITH MISSION AND VALUES

In the end, we want to go back to 30,000 feet and ask: Are our spaces and places serving our mission, vision, and values? In other words, is there intentional alignment of space and mission?

If students are at the center of everything we do (and they should be), we need to start looking at spaces and places through that lens at all times. Researchers using NSSE's current data on student learning note that environmental features focused on student success should (Kuh, Kinzie, Schuh, White & Associates, 2005):

- Demonstrate a commitment to teaching and learning.
- Encourage collaborative learning.

- Facilitate student/faculty interaction outside the classroom.
- Enrich the educational experience through expressed diversity.
- Provide visible and easy access to supportive student services.
- Offer connecting points with the community for campuses committed to supporting their urban neighbors.
- Provide places of solitude on campuses that champion their religious heritage and reflective practices.
- Provide multi-tiered fitness facilities that support health and wellness, and provide facilities for students that would not be available without off-campus financial partnerships.
- Take advantage of the proximity of commercial ventures or shared facilities on campuses that support entrepreneurial partnerships and endeavors.
- Feature science facilities that include exhibits (fish tanks, historical displays, etc.) for campuses that want to connect with their communities.
- Feature concert halls that are accessible to the community, and provide students with multiple performance opportunities.

The right mix of space around us also makes a difference in the quality of our work by affecting real-world performance of professional tasks (Ulrich, 2006). It all comes together when we align people, programs, perception, and place, and design and integrate them all for the purpose of reinforcing the intended experience.

Investment in campus facility planning, or campus master planning, is essential in this new-normal era. We can no longer afford to use the intuition of college administrators when investing millions of dollars to enhance campus. This practice has resulted in many of our campuses looking disjointed or being inconvenient.

Good master planning takes into consideration the strategic initiatives of the college or university, and recommends renovation and building that assist in recruiting and retaining students.

Over the years, I have seen campus master plans take many forms. Not all have been intentionally focused on spaces and places in the context of student learning. As college leaders and administrators, it is our responsibility to be sure that the spaces and places are aligned very carefully with best practice educational and learning pedagogy. When funding is used to place and build buildings without this educational perspective, it is highly likely that the results will not contribute to thriving college success, and may ultimately inhibit it!

It is also common to see beautiful campus master plans that never get implemented. The most successful ones are phased to encourage *action*. The plan itself may include a $10 million solution, but if that funding is not present, it is imperative to begin with $100,000 in small initiatives with big impact. Thriving colleges *always* have a project going. They never settle for waiting, and will always begin with a small project if necessary versus being stagnant until money is available. Improving the environment goes a long way to improving institutional self-esteem. It can reinforce the culture you are trying to build. Doing nothing because you are waiting to do something big is not an option. Creating momentum is critical!

CURB APPEAL AND FIRST IMPRESSIONS

When people drive up to your campus and walk into your buildings, what do they see? You only have one chance to make that first impression (Gladwell, 2007; Willis and Todorov, 2006). Make sure it is a good one. It is important for every college or university community to take small steps in the improvement of curb appeal and first impressions every year.

In 1999, our firm partnered with the Council of Independent Colleges and Disney to create a program for college leaders called *Enhancing the Student Experience* to help our colleges leaders learn to intentionally design *experiences*, not just buildings. Disney makes an unbelievable effort in the first impression arena. We must do the same. We must design this experience perfectly and pay careful attention to that first moment!

When you consider the curb appeal of your campus, remember it is not just about curbs, grass, and buildings. It is about what happens to the heart of a prospective student when he or she drives up to the campus. Broussard (2009) emphasizes that the right use of space can help students to gain a sense of belonging and identity through their first impressions. We have understood for years that if we can help students feel like they belong as soon as possible, our retention rates will go up (Schreiner, Louis, & Nelson, 2012).

It is amazing what happens when the edges of the campus are clearly defined. The *sense of edge* gives identity to the campus, and provides a sense of academic and community space (Blaik, 2007). This is particularly important for an urban campus which needs to find the balance of refuge and energy from the city in which it is located. How it is done is subjective, and reflects the culture of the campus, but it must be done! Many colleges use banners, and others use fencing. A defined edge promotes positive feelings of belonging and engagement:

- I am on the campus now.
- I can navigate this campus.

- I am not afraid.
- I am safe.
- This feels like an oasis to me!

There is not one standard definition of curb appeal, not a picture of another school that would tell you what curb appeal should be at your institution. Your curb appeal is tied up in your institution's identity, vision, and physical place, and can be a part of what makes you truly distinctive. One of our senior master planning consultants related a story to me about a well-defined campus in an urban setting that had focused heavily on their space as a natural habitat. When asked what they loved about their institution, students often mentioned the deer that roamed the campus. Students felt they were a part of nature in that setting, and that was a part of the curb appeal. Other campuses use their history as a part of their physical story, focusing on the richness of their noncontemporary architecture and using it to reinforce their institutional identity. In these cases, old, well-maintained historic buildings scream of permanence and tradition, and they are part of the curb appeal.

IS YOUR WELCOME EXPERIENCE REALLY WELCOMING?

The first impressions of your campus usually happen in a car as people literally drive up to the curb. A campus welcome center in close proximity to guest parking can make a world of difference in that first impression! Although we still often see campus signage directing families to the admissions office, the competition is getting tougher and tougher. The welcome center gives a hospitality edge to the visit experience. It belongs to the guest. It is their space!

Signage is important in bringing cohesion to the welcome experience (Cross, 2007). Just imagine being in a car with the family already anxious about college visits. We always have to remember that the dynamics in that family car are complicated. From the worry about affordability, to the first blush of letting go, this is not an everyday experience. Signage and parking have the ability to make or break the experience. When parking places are marked with the name of the family, there is even a larger sense of belonging.

> From the worry about affordability, to the first blush of letting go, this is not an everyday experience.

While it seems obvious to most, research validates the impact that the physical campus makes on enrollment decisions (Mitchler, 1999). The campus admissions tour is the centerpiece of the visit. It is important for this tour to be carefully and intentionally designed. Thriving colleges storyboard the tour and are very careful about the verbal script and the chosen path. Research tells us that the high point of the admissions tour and the ending point of the tour are the things that people remember most (Baumeister, Bratislavsky, Fickenhauer, & Vohs, 2001). Students are more interested in knowing that they will fit into the experiences on campus rather than understanding the history of buildings.

I've often said that when a tour guide is standing in front of the science building the most compelling statement he or she can make is about the professor inside who is loved or about a class there that was particularly exciting. The training of student ambassadors is essential to the success of any campus visit experience. It is going to be very important for campus administrators to understand the big picture in order to pass this energy and enthusiasm to student ambassadors.

It's important to say that the senior cabinet of a college should actually take the tour each year. It is unbelievable what we notice when we are focused on seeing what our guests see.

TRANSFORMED SPACES ARE JUST AS IMPORTANT AS NEW BUILDINGS!

After touring dozens and dozens of campuses, I am convinced that creativity and open-mindedness play an important role in making the campus facility attractive and appealing. When the focus is on building new buildings, it is awful and immobilizing to a campus that cannot afford those capital projects. We have seen amazing things happen through the transformation of existing spaces. It is essential to keep in mind that attraction, belonging, fit, and commitment are important adjectives when designing and redesigning spaces on campus. Our new and innovative teaching and learning methods are demanding that we embrace more classrooms without walls and add gathering spaces that will promote experiential learning and faculty/student interaction.

We can get much more creative about leveraging current spaces. Some of our best spaces on campus are off-limits to student use. As good stewards, we need to be looking everywhere for the best student-centered space opportunities. These are some of the questions we should be asking ourselves:

- Do we really need more classrooms, or can we get creative about spaces for learning?
- Have we thought enough about "thick" spaces, those that can be used for more than one activity?

- Are we thinking about spaces that can inspire transformational experiences, instead of being focused on decorating those spaces?
- Have we thought about how to transform library spaces into contemporary learning commons areas, with fewer stacks of books and quiet places and more group study, learning support services, food, and chatter?
- Are we thinking about multi-purpose campus centers, so there are spaces that move from food service, to small group gatherings, to large campus community events?
- Is our furniture flexible enough to allow spaces to morph and for learning to take place using different methods?
- How do we think about paint and colors? Is our campus bathed in off-white paint?
- Do you immediately see life in the residence halls when you enter? Are the walls painted with murals that scream about the culture and the identity of students who live there? Are there common spaces that encourage community, and bring learning and living together?

Third Spaces

Part of the success of Starbucks has been its ability to leverage the attributes of the "third space" (Oldenburg, 1999, 2002). A spokesperson for the company describes this phenomenon as "a comfortable, sociable gathering spot away from home and work, like an extension of the front porch" (Walton, 2012; Mehta & Bosson, 2010). Colleges and universities are getting better at designing third spaces with these features. A study found that majors were more popular when the department had space that was highly conducive to interaction between students and faculty (Hilborn, Howes, and Krane, 2003). We have never seen more of a need to expand the opportunities for this type of rich interaction!

Frequently, innovation comes from intentionally creating spaces where brainstorming and conversations lead to new ideas. Colleges and universities across the country should be places where innovative ideas and concepts are born! We must pay careful attention to designing spaces that will encourage that process.

Lastly, as campuses grow, more attention is needed to breaking down spaces in a way that helps to build community. While small campuses generally do this well, growing campuses need to adopt some of these successful strategies. First, campus leaders can brainstorm ways in which there are natural subgroups on campus. These could include majors, departments, affinity groups, partnerships, etc., because they all have some internal psychological cohesion (Schreiner, Miller, Pullins, & Seppelt, 2012). Related to this concept is the development of walkable groupings. An example of this is a grouping of residential colleges that can include both residential use and academic use. While this is becoming common at large universities, the same concepts can be leveraged at smaller colleges and universities (Kaplan & Kaplan, 2004).

WHAT'S NEW IN EDUCATIONAL FACILITY DESIGN?

In decades past, many campuses (especially large publics) were focused on economy and efficiency. While those practices are changing on some campuses, private colleges and university have an opportunity to be leaders in innovation. This innovation can come in the form of visually interesting buildings. Perhaps even more importantly, however, is how college and university leaders can design their campuses to be less siloed and more integrative.

While past practices emphasized siloing spaces into sections of residence halls, academic buildings, and athletic centers, next practices will break down these silos in favor of more flexibility, integration, and collaboration (Harris & Holly, 2008). This collaboration can take many forms. For example, faculty offices and even faculty residences can move into spaces where students live, study, and work. Fusion buildings can bring together single-use space into multi-use space that provides for richer experience and reduced costs. For example, you could blend together an art department, art gallery, student lounge, and coffee shop. This cross-utilization actually increases student engagement in all related venues and reduces costs (Hamilton, 2009).

Next practices will break down silos in favor of more flexibility, integration, and collaboration.

Classrooms can be revisited as well. Remember that science lecture hall with the steep stairs and fixed chairs? Next practices are leading us to active learning classrooms that combine flexible space, technology, stimulating colors, and natural lighting (Brooks, 2010; Cuseo, 2005; Fielding, 2006; Lei, 2010).

An extension of the classroom as a learning commons combines social areas with learning areas. Another feature of these learning commons is the inclusion of spaces that are designed for personal use, team use, and small group use. These multiple formats allow each group size to maximize their contribution to learning in a social setting (Keating & Gabb, 2005).

WHAT ABOUT THOSE RESIDENCE HALLS?

When I'm engaged in a conversation with a college president about the obstacles to recruiting and retention, the residence halls are always a topic of discussion. We have a whole country full of colleges with older residence halls and all of those colleges are dreaming about new ones! It has been a breath of fresh air to see what can happen when those old historical residence halls are renovated.

I asked our campus architectural team at Credo how they would advise a college president to be thinking about the residence halls of the future. Whether you are considering building new housing facilities or renovating the old ones, their response was to pay careful attention to the following things:

- Determine the right sleeping room style and size given the existing configuration of the structure of the building.
- Provide enough collaborative study spaces as well as individual study spaces.
- Provide social environment throughout the building, enough to get students into active communities.
- Provide group cooking opportunities.
- Create an identity for the building as well as the student community.
- Provide enough laundry facilities.
- If the desire is a true teaching and learning environment, provide a faculty apartment large enough for a family and a place to gather with 10–20 students.
- Provide a resident director apartment large enough for a family.
- Design a multi-purpose classroom/tutoring/study space with flexibility and access to the exterior.
- Provide direct access to exterior social and recreational spaces.

It is going to be essential to think more about residential living and learning on every one of our campuses. This is a unique point of difference, and creates amazing leadership opportunities, faculty and student relationships, and traditions that will live and grow.

SUMMARY

If there was ever a need for an external partner, it is in this area of transformative environments. The very best thing a college president can do is choose one partner and build a relationship that will reveal itself in sound educational practices related to the placement of buildings and spaces: designing and implementing experiences, not just pretty buildings. The big picture of a bright future will be the result of this partnership, and will be measured in the long-term by increased enrollments and financial stability.

DISCUSSION QUESTIONS:
TRANSFORMATIVE ENVIRONMENTS

- Does your campus have attractive curb appeal?
- Does your institution have an intentionally designed welcome experience?
- Does your welcome experience tell your story and align with your identity?
- Does your campus invite involvement through logical organization of programs, functions, and activities?
- Does the campus reflect the presence of attractive natural features?

- Are your spaces and places easy to find and navigate?
- Does the campus reflect the presence of clearly defined borders?
- Does the campus reflect the presence of visible activity?
- Does the campus reflect the presence of beautiful views?
- Does the campus reflect the presence of highlighted iconic structures?
- Does the campus reflect the presence of consistent environmental branding?
- Does the campus reflect the presence of a feeling of safety and security?
- Does the campus reflect the presence of good maintenance?
- Do campus spaces and places optimize student success?
- Do campus spaces and places foster diverse forms of social engagement?
- Do campus spaces and places inspire creative approaches to teaching and learning?
- Do the campus spaces and places support best practices in residence life?

Chapter 11

Action
Follows
Belief

What a thrill it has been in the last year of my full-time career to capture the concerns of college presidents, my insights, and current research all in one place. I have loved the journey, and will always be grateful for the opportunity to serve you. My great expectation is that the result of reading this will be *action*! I want to encourage college presidents to press on and embrace the opportunity to thrive.

Although we have addressed many obstacles on the higher education horizon, there is much reason for hope. With good leadership and planning, we can, without doubt, increase the opportunities for private colleges to succeed, and provide transformational moments for the students of today and tomorrow. On our team at Credo, we often say that there is no silver bullet to change institutions, but there are many, many copper ones. We need to identify them and *act*!

I have not attempted in this book to explain the process for every initiative that I noted as essential. I was purposeful in that decision. I want to call you to action. This book is meant to drive you to the places that can help you walk through some of today's challenges and best practices. It is a book written to stimulate discussion in crucial areas. It is because of my thousands of hours on college campuses over these last 15 years that I am aware of the number of conversations that are not pointed at the right issues. It has never been more important for us to focus on what really counts!

My intention is that this book will be useful to college leadership teams and board of trustee members. If you have found it to be helpful, and ascertained that it could be a vehicle for promoting action and movement in your institution, then it should be a common reading for one or both of these identified groups.

The discussion questions at the end of each chapter are meant to alert you to issues of urgency on your campus that need to be addressed. I want these issues to be heard in your planning process, and result in some highly accountable goals that bring your college or university to another level of thriving. I truly believe that discussions around these issues will be more relevant and effective than a SWOT analysis.

And so this journey through a tale of two colleges and 200 more comes to an end, but my sincere hope is that this is the beginning for you! I started the book with the description of myself as a college student with potential. Almost everyone reading this book will resonate with that student – it is the student we love because we can see the light bulb go on, and learning begin. If I leave you with a parting thought, it would be one we have championed throughout the book: teach well the students you have! Spend your time understanding them, plan for them, and be courageous enough to change because of them. It is one of the most energizing times to be an educator. We are challenged by many external forces, but must continue to bring our passion for learning to the right students at the right time. You will need to make difficult decisions, but if you keep students at the center of, and as the motivation for, everything you do, then you will always be walking the right path.

About Credo & the Thriving Framework Inventory

➡ **Learn more: Thriving.CredoHigherEd.com**

ABOUT THE SURVEY

The Thriving Framework Inventory diagnostic tool is a companion survey to this book that allows leadership teams and boards of trustees to evaluate their own institution's level of urgency across the elements of the Thriving Framework. If you purchased this book from Credo's online store or via a Credo project, you should have received an email giving you access to the survey. Survey links are for one use only and are tied to each individual's account. You may purchase additional surveys via that same online store. We hope you will use the report of your results in your team building and planning activities.

Examining Your Survey Results

While the survey can be taken separate from the book, we recommend board and cabinet members read the book before or after taking the survey to set their results into a general context. For a more comprehensive unpacking and examination of your individual or team aggregate results, Credo's experienced consultants can facilitate a planning day for you in our offices. During your time with us, we will share insights about national higher educations trends and best practices related to the survey and the Thriving Framework. We can go into depth with you about any of the elements in which your institution is seeing a high level of urgency, with the goal of priority-setting for the most productive path forward.

ABOUT CREDO

Credo is a higher education consulting firm focused on holistic assessment and action. With knowledge leaders in presidential strategies, student success, enrollment solutions, campus planning and architecture, branding and marketing, and research, Credo has partnered more than 200 institutions across the country.

Credo offers research-driven recommendations, proven processes and practical tools to help your institution thrive. We work hard to understand your culture, invest in your mission and embrace your distinctions in the marketplace. Using our expertise from across the higher education landscape allows us to comprehensively address your challenges while lifting up your opportunities.

Further Endorsements & Valued Partners

In the flurry of books published recently on American higher education, "Surviving to Thriving" is quite simply a must-read for administrators, faculty, staff and trustees. Soliday and Mann present a comprehensive and compelling argument about the distinguishing characteristics of excellent private colleges and universities. Their case is grounded in current literature, and documented with evidence drawn from the wide-ranging experience and expertise of the authors. Strategic questions posed at the end of each chapter invite readers to reflect upon their own organizational realities in light of the larger narrative. If you read only one book on higher education in the months ahead, it should be this one.

— *Dr. Rebecca Sherrick, President, Aurora University*

The beauty of Joanne's writing is that it is easy to read and comprehend, and it provides the guiding path for its readers to find success on their campus. I love her common sense approach provided in a step-by-step guide that includes discussion questions and metrics to help the reader assess their progress. It's practical... it's strategic... it's magic! For those of us who have spent our careers in private colleges and universities, we know that her expertise rings true. She has practiced what she preaches to great effect in her professional life. Now she helps others to achieve similar success.

— *Dr. Dan Carey, President, Edgewood College*

Joanne Soliday has walked alongside me as professional consultant and personal advisor throughout the decade I have served as a college president. Her wisdom, born from deep and broad experience as both student and practitioner in the world of private colleges and universities, was foundational in the beginning turnaround stage of my presidency, and in all the stages moving forward. This book, which will stand as the enduring legacy of Joanne's lifelong vocation, only cements her place as one of the necessary giants in the field. When I am not with Joanne and am trying to address the next short-range or long-range issue on my desk, I often ask myself, "What would Joanne say or do in this situation?" Now I have her book to help me remember as I enter my next decade!

— *Dr. J. Cameron West, President, Huntingdon College*

Want to know what it takes to make your institution thrive? Augmenting their own rich experience with impressive research, Joanne Soliday and Rick Mann have distilled and outlined the key drivers behind successful private colleges and universities. Read their work and profit. I mean, you are making decisions anyway, so you might as well make them smart ones!

— *Dr. Thomas Kunkel, President, St. Norbert College*

As a university president who has benefited from several of the presidential Strategy Days with Joanne Soliday, I can honestly say that this book should be required reading for all college and university leadership. The wealth of knowledge, perspective, and resources available in this volume is priceless, and will provide energy and motivation for creating a roadmap to success.

— *Dr. Gordon Bietz, President, Southern Adventist University*

"Surviving to Thriving" offers board members, presidents, and senior administration a tested and timely virtual roadmap as we lead our private institutions. This resource will become a valuable tool in that it offers comprehensive, insightful, experiential observations combined with sound higher educational research. It has relevance to the current higher educational environment and concisely articulates the leadership characteristics instrumental in building an enduring organization.

— *Dr. Bill Johnston, President, Wesley College*

"Surviving to Thriving" is a must-read for senior-level administrators and trustees at small, private colleges. Joanne Soliday is an astute observer of higher education, and she is passionate about her work with small colleges that spans more than three decades. She and Rick Mann deliver truly practical advice based on best practices and sound strategies, and they offer concrete ideas for institutional leaders to take action. Their book is vitally important for understanding what an institution must do to thrive rather than just survive in the current marketplace of higher education.

— *Dr. William T. Abare, Jr., President, Flagler College*

A clear, precise and effective blueprint for planning for success in higher education, "Surviving to Thriving" is a must read for university leaders. We are using these principles and they work.

— *Dr. Dick Geise, President, University of Mount Union*

With confusion, uncertainty and even fear occupying much of higher education, Joanne Soliday has cleared the fog and provided a framework for success. The formula she lays out is detailed and by no means a quick, easy fix. But following it can mean the difference between failure and triumph. This book is filled with commonsense, astute observations, keen analysis and difficult choices. It reflects Soliday's years of experience as an academic leader and a wise and thoughtful educational consultant.

— *Dr. Joseph S. Brosnan, President, Delaware Valley College*

Colleges and universities are challenged today on all fronts, from public opinion to government policy to available financial aid. Few books on the topic of leadership excellence for private colleges and universities have been written more effectively than Joanne Soliday and Rick Mann's book on planning for leaders in private colleges and universities. The book is a valuable collection of observations, stories, findings, and strategies that will help guide all leaders of private higher education from admissions professionals to presidents. "Surviving To Thriving" is an important book for higher education leaders who wish to transform their institutions. "Surviving To Thriving" may become the "Good To Great" for private higher education.

— *Dr. Kevin J. Manning, President, Stevenson University*

To know and work with Joanne Soliday is to know and work with a consummate professional who brings her passion for mission-driven higher education to a campus community – leading the campus through evolution and transformation with style, grace, respect, and dignity. Joanne's recent impact on Neumann University and its strategic plan for the future will be evident for years to come. As importantly, her wisdom, versatility, and vision are instrumental now in bringing excitement and energy for change among all who are involved in leading this process.

— *Dr. Rosalie Mirenda, President, Neumann University*

What Presidents are Reading

Alfred, R. (2006). *Managing the big picture in colleges and universities: From tactical to strategic.* Westpoint, CT: Praeger.

Archibald, R. B. (2011). *Why does college cost so much?* New York, NY: Oxford University Press.

Arum, R., & Roksa, J. (2011). *Academically adrift: Limited learning on college campuses.* Chicago, IL: University of Chicago Press.

Bok, D. C. (2013). *Higher education in America.* Princeton, NJ: Princeton University Press.

Bolman, L., & Gallos, J. (2011). *Reframing academic leadership.* San Francisco, CA: Jossey-Bass.

Bowen, W. G. (2013). *Higher education in the digital age.* Princeton, NJ: Princeton University Press.

Chabotar, K. J. (2006). *Strategic finance: Planning and budgeting for boards, chief executives, and finance officers.* Washington, DC: Association of Governing Boards of Universities and Colleges.

Christensen, C. M., & Eyring, H. J. (2011). *The innovative university: Changing the DNA of higher education from the inside out.* San Francisco, CA: Jossey-Bass.

Collins, K. M., & Roberts, D. M. (2012). *Learning is not a sprint: Assessing and documenting student leader learning in cocurricular involvement.* Washington, DC: National Association of Student Personnel Administrators.

Delbanco, A. (2013). *College: What it was, is, and should be.* Princeton, NJ: Princeton University Press.

Edmundson, M. (2013). *Why teach?: In defense of a real education.* New York, NY: Bloomsbury.

Gladwell, M. (2007). *Blink: The power of thinking without thinking.* New York, NY: Back Bay Books.

Keeling, R. P. (2004). *Learning reconsidered: A campus-wide focus on the student experience.* National Association of Student Personnel Administrators.

Kenney, D. R. (2005). *Mission and place: Strengthening learning and community through campus design.* Westport, CN: Praeger Publishers.

Kezar, A. J. (2013). *How colleges change: Understanding, leading, and enacting change.* New York, NY: Rutledge.

Kirp, D. L. (2004). *Shakespeare, Einstein and the bottom line: The marketing of higher education.* Cambridge, MA: Harvard University Press.

Kotter, J. (2008). *A sense of urgency.* Boston, MA: Harvard Business Press.

Kotter, J. (2012). *Leading change.* Boston, MA: Harvard Business Review Press.

Lagemann, E. C., & Lewis, H. R. (2012). *What is college for?: The public purpose of higher education.* New York, NY: Teachers College Press.

Lencioni, P. (2002). *The five dysfunctions of a team: A leadership fable.* San Francisco, CA: Jossey-Bass.

Lencioni, P. (2004). *Death by meeting: A leadership fable... About solving the most painful problem in business.* San Francisco, CA: Jossey-Bass.

Lencioni, P. (2012). *The advantage: Why organizational health trumps everything else in business.* San Francisco, CA: Jossey-Bass.

Levine, A., & Dean, D. R. (2012). *Generation on a tightrope: A portrait of today's college student.* San Francisco, CA: Jossey-Bass.

Light, R. J. (2004). *Making the most of college: Students speak their minds.* Cambridge, MA: Harvard University Press.

MacTaggart, T. (2011). *Leading change: How boards and presidents build exceptional academic institutions.* Washington, DC: AGB Press.

MacTaggert, T. (2007). *Academic turnarounds: Restoring vitality to the challenged American colleges and universities.* Westpoint, CT: Praeger.

Martin, J., & Samels, J. E. (2009). *Turnaround: Leading stressed colleges and universities to excellence.* Baltimore, MD: Johns Hopkins University Press.

Pascarella, E. T., & Terenzini, P. T. (2005). *How college affects students.* San Francisco, CA: Jossey-Bass.

Pierce, S. R. (2012). *On being presidential: A guide for college and university leaders.* San Francisco, CA: Jossey-Bass.

Sample, S. B. (2003). *The contrarian's guide to leadership.* San Francisco, CA: Jossey-Bass.

Sandberg, S. (2013). *Lean in: Women, work, and the will to lead.* New York, NY: Alfred A. Knopf.

Schreiner, L. A., Louis, M. C., & Nelson, D. D. (2012). *Thriving in transitions: A research-based approach to college student success.* Columbia, SC: University of South Carolina, National Resource Center for the First-Year Experience and Students in Transition.

Selingo, J. J. (2013). *College (un)bound: The future of higher education and what it means for students.* Boston, MA: Houghton Mifflin Harcourt.

Sinek, S. (2009). *Start with why: How great leaders inspire everyone to take action.* New York, NY: Portfolio.

Vedder, R. K. (2004). *Going broke by degree: Why college costs too much.* Washington, DC: AEI Press.

References

Abelman, R., & Dalessandro, A. (2009). Institutional vision in Christian higher education: A comparison of ACCCU, ELCA, and CCCU institutions. *Journal of Research on Christian Education, 18*(1), 84–119.

ACT. (2010). What works in student retention? Retrieved from https://www.act.org/research/policymakers/pdf/droptables/AllInstitutions.pdf

Alfred, R. (2006). *Managing the big picture in colleges and universities: From tactical to strategic.* Westpoint, CT: Praeger.

Anderson, J. C., Narus, J. A., & van Rossum, W. (2006). Customer value propositions in business markets. *Harvard Business Review, 84*(3), 90–99.

Association of Governing Boards of Universities and Colleges. (2012a). *Effective governing boards: A guide for members of governing boards of independent colleges and universities.* Washington, DC: AGB Press.

Association of Governing Boards of Universities and Colleges. (2012b). The 2012 AGB survey of higher education governance. College prices, costs, and outcomes: Who's minding the gap between higher education and the public? Retrieved from http://agb.org/reports/2012/2012-agb-survey-higher-education-governance

Bartlett, T., & Fischer, K. (2011, November 3). The China conundrum. *The Chronicle of Higher Education.* Retrieved from http://chronicle.com/article/Chinese-Students-Prove-a/129628/

Basken, P. (2012, May 17). Quest for college accountability produces demand for yet more student data. *The Chronicle of Higher Education.* Retrieved from http://chronicle.com/article/Quest-for-College/131910/

Baumeister, R., Bratislavsky, E., Fickenhauer, C., & Vohs, D. (2001). Bad is stronger than good. *Review of General Psychology, 5,* 323–370.

Bichsel, J. (2012). Analytics in Higher Education: Benefits, Barriers, Progress, and Recommendations. EDUCAUSE Center for Applied Research. Retrieved from http://www.educause.edu/library/resources/2012-ecar-study-analytics-higher-education

Bips, L. (2010). Students are different now - room for debate. *The New York Times.* Retrieved from http://www.nytimes.com/roomfordebate/2010/10/11/have-college-freshmen-changed/students-are-different-now

Blaik, O. (2007). Campuses in cities: Places between engagement and retreat. *The Chronicle of Higher Education.* Retrieved from http://chronicle.com/article/Campuses-in-Cities-Places/27584/

Bonwell, C. C., & Eison, J. A. (1991). *Active learning: Creating excitement in the classroom.* San Francisco, CA: Jossey-Bass.

Brooks, D. (2010). Space matters: The impact of formal learning environments on student learning. *British Journal of Educational Technology.* Retrieved from http://www.oit.umn.edu/prod/groups/oit/@pub/@oit/@web/@evaluationresearch/documents/article/oit_article_248303.pdf

Broussard, E. (2009). The power of place on campus. *The Chronicle of Higher Education.* Retrieved from http://chronicle.com/article/The-Power-of-Place-on-Campus/3399/

Bryson, J. M. (2010). The future of public and nonprofit strategic planning in the United States. *Public Administration Review,* 70, s255–s267. doi:10.1111/j.1540-6210.2010.02285.x

Bryson, J. M. (2011). *Strategic planning for public and nonprofit organizations: A guide to strengthening and sustaining organizational achievement.* San Francisco, CA: Jossey-Bass. Retrieved from http://site.ebrary.com/id/10483249

Cady, S. H., Wheeler, J. V., DeWolf, J., & Brodke, M. (2011). Mission, vision, and values: What do they say? *Organization Development Journal,* 29(1), 63–78.

Cardoso Vieira Machado, M. J. (2013). Balanced Scorecard: An empirical study of
small and medium size enterprises. *Review of Business Management*, 15(46),
129–148. doi:10.7819/rbgn.v15i46.1175

Carlson, S. (2013, April 22). How to assess the real payoff of a college degree. *The
Chronicle of Higher Education*. Retrieved from http://chronicle.com/article/Is-ROI-
the-Right-Way-to-Judge/138665/

Carver, J., & Carver, M. M. (2006). *Reinventing your board: A step-by-step guide to
implementing policy governance*. San Francisco, CA: John Wiley.

Chickering, A., & Gamson, Z. (1987). *Seven principles for good practice in undergraduate
education*. Washington, D.C.: American Association of Higher Education.

Christensen, C. M., Horn, M. B., & Soares, L. (2011). *Disrupting college*. Center for
American Progress. Retrieved from http://www.americanprogress.org/issues/
labor/report/2011/02/08/9034/disrupting-college/

Christesen, D. A. (2008). *The impact of balanced scorecard usage on organization
performance* (Doctoral dissertation). University of Minnesota. Minneapolis, MN.
Retrieved from http://search.proquest.com.ezp.waldenulibrary.org/pqcentral/
docview/304595608/abstract/13FB1B878DD6549D7/8?accountid=14872

Clifton, J. D. (2003). *An analysis of mission statement consistency with curricular offerings
in liberal arts colleges accredited by the Southern Association of Colleges and Schools*
(Doctoral dissertation). Texas Tech University. Lubbock, TX. Retrieved from
http://0-search.proquest.com.library.trevecca.edu/docview/305297903/abstract/1
4088CEAF5341B6BDB4/9?accountid=29083

Collins, J. C., & Porras, J. I. (1994). *Built to last: Successful habits of visionary companies*.
New York, NY: HarperBusiness.

Coutu, D., & Beschloss, M. (2009). Why teams don't work. *Harvard Business Review*,
87(5), 98–105.

Cuseo, J. (2005). The empirical case against large class size: Adverse effects on teaching, learning, and retention of first-year students. *Journal of Faculty Development, 21*(1), 5–21.

Davenport, T. H. (2013). Keep Up with Your Quants. *Harvard Business Review, 91*(7), 120–123.

De Pree, M. (1989). *Leadership is an art.* New York, NY: Doubleday.

De Jong, B., & Elfring, T. (2010). How does trust affect the performance of ongoing teams? The mediating role of reflexivity, monitoring, and effort. *Academy of Management Journal, 53*(3), 535–549. doi:10.5465/AMJ.2010.51468649

Derilhomme Joasil, L. G. (2008). *A study into the relationship between observed and model values of men and women leaders in higher education* (Doctoral dissertation). Capella University. Minneapolis, MN. Retrieved from http://0-search.proquest.com. library.trevecca.edu/docview/219980997/abstract/14088BEB0464F186920/6?acc ountid=29083

Doren, M. V. (1943). *Liberal education.* New York, NY: Henry Holt and Company.

Duncan, A. (2009). Robust data gives us the roadmap to reform. Presentation at the Fourth Annual IES Research Conference, Washington, DC. Retrieved from http://www.ed.gov/news/speeches/robust-data-gives-us-roadmap-reform

Eaton, J. S. (2010). Accreditation and the Federal Future of Higher Education. *Academe, 96*(5), 21–24.

Eaton, J. S. (2012). The Future of Accreditation. *Planning for Higher Education, 40*(3), 8–15.

Edelman, D. C. (2010). Branding in the digital age. *Harvard Business Review, 88*(12), 62–69.

Fain, P. (2009, May 1). Few governing boards engage in sophisticated financial planning, experts say. *The Chronicle of Higher Education.* Retrieved from http:// chronicle.com/article/Few-Governing-Boards-Engage-in/1876/

Fielden, J. (2010, July 18). Leading international partnerships: 7 roles for presidents. *The Chronicle of Higher Education.* Retrieved from http://chronicle.com/article/Leading-International/66310/

Fielding, R. (2006). Learning, lighting, and color: Lighting design for schools and universities in the 21st century. *Professional Lighting Design.* Retrieved from www.designshare.com/articles/1/133/fielding_light-learn-color.pdf

Flandez, R. (2012). The cost of high turnover in fundraising jobs. *The Chronicle of Philanthropy.* Retrieved from http://philanthropy.com/blogs/prospecting/the-cost-of-high-turnover-in-fundraising-jobs/32752

Friedman, J. (2013, June 17). Nine "no confidence" votes that made headlines in 2012-2013. *Huffington Post.* Retrieved from http://www.huffingtonpost.com/jordan-friedman/nine-no-confidence-votes-_b_3448606.html

Fullan, M., & Scott, G. (2009). *Turnaround leadership for higher education.* San Francisco, CA: Jossey-Bass.

Garvey, C. (2005). Philosophizing compensation. *HR Magazine, 50*(1), 73–76.

Gladwell, M. (2007). *Blink: The power of thinking without thinking.* New York, NY: Back Bay Books.

Greatbanks, R., & Tapp, D. (2007). The impact of balanced scorecards in a public sector environment: Empirical evidence from Dunedin City Council, New Zealand. *International Journal of Operations & Production Management, 27*(8), 846.

Green, K. (2011). Presidential perspectives: The 2011 Inside Higher Ed survey of college and university presidents. *Inside Higher Ed.* Retrieved from http://www.insidehighered.com/sites/default/archive/storage/files/SurveyBooklet.pdf

Griggs, V., Blackburn, M., & Smith, J. (2012). The Educational Scorecard: The Start of our Journey. *Electronic Journal of Business Research Methods, 10*(2), 121–131.

Guan, J., Nunez, W., & Welsh, J. F. (2002). Institutional strategy and information support: The role of data warehousing in higher education. *Campus - Wide Information Systems, 19*(5), 168–174.

Habley, W. R., Bloom, J. L., & Robbins, S. (2012). *Increasing persistence: Research-based strategies for college student success.* San Francisco, CA: Jossey-Bass.

Halvorson, H. (2011). *Nine things successful people do differently.* Cambridge, MA: Harvard Business Review Press.

Hamilton, C. (2009). Fusion building: New trend with some old roots. *Planning for Higher Education, 37*(2), 44–51.

Harris, M., & Holley, K. (2008). Constructing the interdisciplinary ivory tower: The planning of interdisciplinary spaces on university campuses. *Planning for Higher Education, 36*(3), 34–43.

Hartley, H., & Godin, E. (2009). A study of career patterns of the presidents of independent colleges and universities. Council of Independent Colleges. Retrieved from http://www.cic.org/Research-and-Data/Research-Studies/Documents/CICPresSurvey.pdf

Hebel, S. (2008). Higher education's grade for data: "Incomplete." *The Chronicle of Higher Education, 55*(16). Retrieved from http://chronicle.com/article/Higher-Educations-Grade-for/1387

Hilborn, R., Howes, R., & Krane, K. (2003). *Strategic programs for innovations in undergraduate physics: Project report.* College Park, MD: The American Association of Physics Teachers.

Hill, A. (2013). How to create values, vision, and missions statements. Clamshell Beach Press.

Hoover, E. (2010, April 27). On transfer students and transfer-friendliness. *Head Count.* The Chronicle of Higher Education. Retrieved from http://chronicle.com/blogs/headcount/on-transfer-studentstransfer-friendliness/23499

Hoover, E. (2011, May 15). College's value goes deeper than the degree, graduates say. *The Chronicle of Higher Education.* Retrieved from http://chronicle.com/article/Its-More-Than-Just-the/127534/

Hoover, E., & Supiano, B. (2013, September 16). In admissions, old playbook is being

revised. *The Chronicle of Higher Education*. Retrieved from http://chronicle.com/

article/The-Admissions-Playbook-Is-Up/141625/

Hunter, J. M. (2012). *An integrated framework for understanding the financial health

of small, private colleges* (Doctoral dissertation). University of Minnesota.

Minneapolis, MN. Retrieved from www.proquest.com

Ibarra, H., & Hansen, M. T. (2011). Are you a collaborative leader? *Harvard Business

Review*, 89(7/8), 68–74.

Jaschik, S. (2013). Jobs, value and affirmative action: A survey of parents about

college. *Inside Higher Ed*. Retrieved from http://www.insidehighered.com/news/

survey/jobs-value-and-affirmative-action-survey-parents-about-college

June, A. (2013). How administrators define success. *The Chronicle of Higher

Education*. Retrieved from http://chronicle.com/article/How-Administrators-

Measure/140419/

Kaplan, R., & Norton, D. (2008). *The execution premium*. Cambridge, MA: Harvard

Business School Press.

Katz, D. L. (2010). Dismantling silos of uncooperative teams. *CIO Insight*, (113), 12–14.

Katz, S. (2009, July 27). Assessment in Higher Ed. *Brainstorm*. The Chronicle of

Higher Education. Retrieved from http://chronicle.com/blogs/brainstorm/

assessment-in-higher-ed/7489

Keating, S., & Gabb, R. (2005). *Putting learning in the learning commons. A literature

review*. Victoria University. Melbourne, Australia. Retrieved from http://vuir.

vu.edu.au/94/

Kelderman, E. (2013, February 13). Obama's accreditation proposals surprise higher-

education leaders. *The Chronicle of Higher Education*. Retrieved from http://

chronicle.com/article/Obamas-Accreditation/137311/

Keller, G. (1983). *Academic strategy: The management revolution in American higher

education*. Baltimore, MD: Johns Hopkins University Press.

Keller, G. (2004). *Transforming a college: the story of a little-known college's strategic climb to national distinction.* Baltimore, MD: Johns Hopkins University Press.

Keller, K. L. (2000). The brand report card. *Harvard Business Review, 78*(1), 147–157.

Keller, K. L. (2012). *Strategic brand management.* Upper Saddle River, NJ: Prentice Hall.

Kotter, J. (1990). What leaders really do. *Harvard Business Review, 68*(3), 103–111.

Kotter, J. (2007). Leading change: Why transformation efforts fail. *Harvard Business Review, 85*(1), 96–103.

Kotter, J. (2008). *A sense of urgency.* Boston, MA: Harvard Business Press.

Kotter, J. (2012). *Leading change.* Boston, MA: Harvard Business Review Press.

Krachenberg, A. (1972). Bringing the concept of marketing to higher education. *The Journal of Higher Education, 43*(5), 369–380.

Kuh, G. (2008). High impact educational practices. Association of American Colleges and Universities. Retrieved from http://www.neasc.org/downloads/aacu_high_impact_2008_final.pdf

Kuh, G., Kinzie, J., Schuh, J., & Whitt, E. (2005). *Student success in college: Creating conditions that matter.* San Francisco, CA: Jossey-Bass.

Kvavik, R., & Handburg, M. (2000). Transforming student services. *Educause Quarterly, 2,* 30–37.

LaFrance, S., & Latham, N. (2008, Summer). Taking stock of venture philanthropy. *Stanford Social Innovation Review, 6*(3), 60–65.

Lanning, P. I. (2007). *Developing expertise in higher education fundraising: A conceptual framework* (Doctoral dissertation). University of the Pacific. Stockton, CA. Retrieved from http://o-search.proquest.com.library.trevecca.edu/docview/304820702/abstract/1409EE465E62E1A0745/2?accountid=29083

Lederer, C., & Hill, S. (2001). See your brands through your customers' eyes. *Harvard Business Review, 79*(6), 125–133.

Lederman, D. (2009, November 18). Defining Accountability. *Inside Higher Ed.* Retrieved from http://www.insidehighered.com/news/2009/11/18/aei

Lei, S. (2010). Classroom physical design influencing student learning and evaluations of college instructors: A review of literature. *Education*, 131(1), 128–134.

Lencioni, P. (2002a). Make your values mean something. *Harvard Business Review*, 80(7), 113–117.

Lencioni, P. (2002b). *The five dysfunctions of a team: A leadership fable*. San Francisco, CA: Jossey-Bass.

Lencioni, P. (2004). *Death by meeting: A leadership fable... About solving the most painful problem in business*. San Francisco, CA: Jossey-Bass.

Lencioni, P. (2006). *Silos, politics, and turf wars: A leadership fable about destroying the barriers that turn colleagues into competitors*. San Francisco, CA: Jossey-Bass.

Lencioni, P. (2012). *The advantage: Why organizational health trumps everything else in business*. San Francisco, CA: Jossey-Bass.

Leveille, D. (2005). *An emerging view on accountability in American higher education*. Center for Studies in Higher Education. Retrieved from http://cshe.berkeley.edu/publications/publications.php?id=54

Levine, A., & Dean, D. R. (2012). *Generation on a tightrope: A portrait of today's college student*. San Francisco, CA: Jossey-Bass.

Linton, M. (2009, May 15). Why do chief marketing officers have a short shelf life? *Forbes*. Retrieved from http://www.forbes.com/2009/05/15/cmo-turnover-dilemma-cmo-network-dilemma.html

Lipka, S. (2013, August 15). Despite financial concerns, most parents still value college. *Head Count*. The Chronicle of Higher Education. Retrieved from http://chronicle.com/blogs/headcount/despite-financial-concerns-most-parents-still-value-college/36133

Lopez, S. J. (2013). *Making hope happen: Create the future you want for yourself and others*. New York, NY: Atria Books.

Lorinkova, N. M., Pearsall, M. J., & Sims, Jr., H. P. (2013). Examining the differential longitudinal performance of directive versus empowering leadership in teams. *Academy of Management Journal, 56*(2), 573–596. doi:10.5465/amj.2011.0132

Lunger, K. (2006). Why you need more than a dashboard to manage your strategy. *Business Intelligence Journal, 11*(4), 8–17.

MacTaggert, T. (2007). *Academic turnarounds: Restoring vitality to the challenged American colleges and universities.* Westpoint, CT: Praeger.

Martin, J., & Samels, J. E. (2009). *Turnaround: Leading stressed colleges and universities to excellence.* Baltimore, MD: Johns Hopkins University Press.

Maslowsky, C. (2013). Five ways higher education marketing will change in 10 years. *Evolllution.com.* Retrieved from http://www.evolllution.com/opinions/ways-higher-education-marketing-change-10-years/

Meacham, J. (2008). What's the use of a mission statement? *Academe, 94*(1), 21–24.

Mehta, V., & Bosson, J. (2010). Third places and the social life of streets. *Environment and Behavior, 42*(6), 779–805.

Mitchler, A. (1999). *Atmospherics and the campus visit.* Credo White Paper.

Mrozinski, M. D. (2010). *Multiple roles: The conflicted realities of community college mission statements* (Doctoral dissertation). National-Louis University. Chicago, IL. Retrieved from http://0-search.proquest.com.library.trevecca.edu/docview/502056543/abstract/14075B96F43DCB3A57/44?accountid=29083

National Association of College and University Business Officers. (2013). Getting started on benchmarking. Retrieved from http://www.nacubo.org/Research/Benchmarking_Resources.html

Nicklin, J. L. (1998, September 25). Revolving doors in development offices. *The Chronicle of Higher Education.* Retrieved from http://chronicle.com/article/Revolving-Doors-in-Development/14367/

Niven, P. R. (2008). *Balanced scorecard step-by-step for government and nonprofit agencies.* Hoboken, NJ: J. Wiley & Sons.

O'Hearn, C. C. (2004). *The mission statement and planning in California community colleges* (Doctoral dissertation). Capella University. Minneapolis, MN. Retrieved from http://search.proquest.com.ezp.waldenulibrary.org/docview/305041225/ab stract/1415BC8268070B192F1/1?accountid=14872

Oldenburg, R. (1999). *The great good place*. Philadelphia, PA: Da Capo.

Oldenburg, R. (2002). The "third place": Essential for campuses and communities. *The Lawlor Review.* Retrieved from http://www.thelawlorgroup.com/pov/review/ archives-pdf

Pascarella, E. T., & Terenzini, P. T. (2005). *How college affects students*. San Francisco, CA: Jossey-Bass.

Peale, C. (2013). Small colleges use sports to boost the bottom line. *Cincinnati. com.* Retrieved from http://news.cincinnati.com/article/20130916/ NEWS0102/309160030/Small-colleges-use-sports-boost-bottom-line

Porter, M. E. (1996). What is strategy? *Harvard Business Review*, 74(6), 61–78.

Pullaro, N. (2012). Cost of undergraduate recruitment at four-year institutions has held steady since 2009. National Association of College and University Business Officers. Retrieved from http://www.nacubo.org/Research/Research_ News/Cost_of_Undergraduate_Recruitment_at_Four-year_institutions_Has_ Held_Steady_Since_2009.html

Pulley, J. L. (2003, October 24). Romancing the brand. *The Chronicle of Higher Education.* Retrieved from http://chronicle.com/article/Romancing-the-Brand/2712/

Raisman, N. (2009). Retain students retain budgets: A how. To. *University Business.* Retrieved from http://www.universitybusiness.com/article/retain-students-retain-budgets-how

Raynor, M. E., & Ahmed, M. (2013). Three rules for making a company really great. *Harvard Business Review*, 91(4), 108–117.

Rigby, D., & Bilodeau, B. (2011). *Management tools and trends: 2011*. Boston, MA: Bain and Company.

Rohm, H. (2008). Is there any strategy in your strategic plan? Balanced Scorecard
Institute. Retrieved from http://www.balancedscorecard.org/Portals/0/PDF/
IsThereAnyStrategyInYourStrategicPlanWeb.pdf

Rothwell, W. J. (2010). *Effective succession planning: Ensuring leadership continuity and
building talent from within.* New York, NY: AMACOM.

Saltman, K. J. (2010). *The gift of education: public education and venture philanthropy.* New
York, NY: Palgrave Macmillan.

Schreiner, L. A., Louis, M. C., & Nelson, D. D. (2012). *Thriving in transitions: A research-
based approach to college student success.* Columbia, SC: University of South
Carolina, National Resource Center for the First-Year Experience and Students
in Transition.

Schreiner, L. A., Miller, L., Pullins, T., & Seppelt, T. (2012). Beyond sophomore
survival. In Schreiner, L.A., Louis, M.C. & Nelson, D.D. (Eds.) *Thriving in
transitions: A research based approach to college student success.* Columbia, SC:
University of South Carolina, National Resource Center for the First-Year
Experience and Students in Transition.

Schreiner, L. A., Noel, P., Anderson, E. "Chip", & Cantwell, L. (2011). The impact of
faculty and staff on high-risk college student persistence. *Journal of College
Student Development, 52*(3), 321–338.

Selingo, J. (2012, March 8). The Student Swirl. *Next.* The Chronicle of Higher
Education. Retrieved from http://chronicle.com/blogs/next/2012/03/08/the-
student-swirl/

Shields, T. (2007). Board development: Governing boards as communities of practice.
The International Journal of Learning, 14(5), 89–95.

Shrader, C. B., Taylor, L., & Dalton, D. R. (1984). Strategic planning and organizational
performance: A critical appraisal. *Journal of Management, 10*(2), 149–171.

Shushok, F., Henry, D., Blalock, G., & Sriram, R. (2009). Learning at any time:
Supporting student learning wherever it happens. *About Campus, 14*(1), 10–15.

Simon, C. C. (2012, November 2). Choosing one college major out of hundreds. *The New York Times*. Retrieved from http://www.nytimes.com/2012/11/04/education/edlife/choosing-one-college-major-out-of-hundreds.html

Song, W., & Hartley, H. (2012). *A study of presidents of independent colleges and universities*. Washington, DC: Council of Independent Colleges and Universities.

Supiano, B. (2009, November 1). Colleges move to organize their retention efforts. *The Chronicle of Higher Education*. Retrieved from http://chronicle.com/article/Colleges-Move-to-Organize/48998/

Supiano, B. (2012, September 19). Students need better information on earnings and other college outcomes, senators say. *The Chronicle of Higher Education*. Retrieved from http://chronicle.com/article/Senators-Seek-to-Shed-Light-on/134536/

Supiano, B. (2013, February 12). With Financial Aid, Colleges Should Be Accountable to Taxpayers and Students, Paper Argues. *The Chronicle of Higher Education*. Retrieved from http://chronicle.com/article/Make-Colleges-More-Accountable/137257/

Tankersley, J. (2013). Starting college? Here's how to graduate with a job. *The Washington Post*. Retrieved from http://articles.washingtonpost.com/2013-08-09/lifestyle/41218827_1_so-called-stem-science-job-market

The White House. (n.d.). *Higher Education*. Retrieved from http://www.whitehouse.gov/issues/education/higher-education

Townsley, M. (2009). *Small college guide to financial health: Weathering turbulent times*. Washington, DC: NACUBO.

Vedder, R. K. (2004). *Going broke by degree: Why college costs too much*. Washington, DC: AEI Press.

Walton, A. (2012, May 29). Starbucks' power over us is bigger than coffee: It's personal. *Forbes*. Retrieved from http://www.forbes.com/sites/alicegwalton/2012/05/29/starbucks-hold-on-us-is-bigger-than-coffee-its-psychology/

Welsh, J. F., Nunez, W. J., & Petrosko, J. (2005). Faculty and administrative support for strategic planning: A comparison of two- and four-year institutions. *Community College Review*, 32(4), 20–39.

Willis, J., & Todorov, A. (2006). First impressions: making up your mind after a 100-ms exposure to a face. *Psychological Science*, 17(7), 592–598.

Young, J. R. (2012, June 25). A conversation with Bill Gates about the future of higher education. *The Chronicle of Higher Education*. Retrieved from http://chronicle.com/article/A-Conversation-With-Bill-Gates/132591/

Zipper, T. (2013, April 3). Making the most of your marketing budget: Is outsourcing the answer? *The Online Learning Curve*. Retrieved from http://www.learninghouse.com/blog/marketing/making-the-most-of-your-marketing-budget-is-outsourcing-the-answer